HIGHER BOND YIELDS

THE TRIPLE-A ADVANTAGE OF INSURED MUNICIPAL BONDS

HIGHER BOND YIELDS

THE TRIPLE-A ADVANTAGE OF INSURED MUNICIPAL BONDS

Robert R. Godfrey
with
Diana L. York

IRWIN
Professional Publishing
Burr Ridge, Illinois
New York, New York

Project editor: Susan Trentacosti
Production manager: Laurie Kersch
Designer: Heidi J. Baughman
Compositor: Eastern Composition, Inc.
Typeface: 11/13 Times Roman
Printer: Arcata Graphics/Kingsport

Library of Congress Cataloging-in-Publication Data

Godfrey, Robert (Robert Ross)
Higher bond yields : the triple-A advantage of insured municipal bonds / by Robert R. Godfrey with Diana L. York.
p. cm.
Includes bibliographical references and index.
ISBN 0-7863-0232-1
1. Municipal bonds—United States. 2. Municipal bonds—Rating—United States. I. York, Diana L. II. Title.
HG4952.G626 1994
322.63'233'0973—dc20 93-34385

Printed in the United States of America
1 2 3 4 5 6 7 8 9 0 AGK 0 9 8 7 6 5 4 3

ACKNOWLEDGMENTS

All projects of this nature require a "cast of thousands" for their completion. I would like to take this opportunity to thank them all and chronicle their assistance.

For getting the mountains of data, doing research, and providing computer assistance: Marc Cahn, Angela Grassi, Brian Hynes, Peg Kroll, Siroui Mushegian, Kimberly Osgood, Rich Quimby, Kevin Regan, Tom Scherer, and Mary Warde.

For analyzing and describing the uninsured credit rating process and the placement ratio: Neil Budnick, William Condon, and Thomas Landers.

Thanks for special administrative help goes to Arlene Altomare and Judy Radasch.

For computerizing the stress test model and teaching others how to use it, as well as a belated thanks for assistance on my first book: Deborah Smith.

Special thanks to my assistant Denise Lehman for not only gathering data, but also running stress tests and typing manuscripts (and keeping a sense of humor while doing it). Many typing thanks also to Judy Cavino, Venetia Heintz, and Maureen Gilmartin. Artwork appreciation goes to Kelly Fego.

For insightful yet diplomatic editing: Bill Bailey and Paul O'Shea.

For critical, academic review: Dr. Edward I. Altman of New York University, the best fixed income academic in the world today.

Last of all to my all-around assistant and coauthor Diana York, thanks for the government bond market chapter and the history of bond insurance, plus the many hours of checking, proofreading, and the assembly and updating of data.

Robert Godfrey

LIST OF FIGURES

ABOUT THE AUTHORS

Robert R. Godfrey

Robert R. Godfrey is executive vice president of the research and business development division of Municipal Bond Investors Assurance Corporation and a member of the firm's Senior Management Committee. This is his second book, as he is also the author of *Risk Based Capital Charges for Municipal Bonds* (Greenwich, CT: JAI Press, 1990). It is the first book in 20 years which comprehensively analyzes municipal bond safety, develops new economic models for testing bond strength, and chronicles defaults over the last 120 years.

During his business career, Mr. Godfrey has served as an advisor to major industrial corporations as well as government and industry associations on management and financial matters. He has also frequently appeared on CNN, FNN/CNBC, and other television and radio business shows in Chicago, Los Angeles, New York, Arizona, and Florida. Robert is also a trustee of the Citizens Budget Commission of New York and a director of the New York University Salomon Center Corporate Advisory Council.

Prior to joining MBIA in 1985, Mr. Godfrey was founder, president, and chief executive officer of St. Regis Insurance Group, the major credit insurer in the U.S. market in the early 1980s. From 1979 to 1981 he served as president and chief operating officer of Rollins Burdick Hunter Management, Inc. Mr. Godfrey began his business career in 1969 at Aetna Life and Casualty after graduating from Texas Tech University.

Diana L. York

Diana L. York is assistant vice president in MBIA's market research department. She earned a bachelor of science degree in business administration in 1984 from the State University of New York at Albany.

CONTENTS

INTRODUCTION

Bond market observers have for years known that similar bonds have different yields, even with the same credit ratings. While studies over the past 40 years have examined this phenomenon, not one has addressed the yield disparity among Triple-A municipal bonds.

Among municipals, yields differ most between the "natural" Triple-A's, which gained the rating on their own merits, and the growing number of issues that buy their Triple-A rating from a bond insurance company. Currently, the yield on an insured 30-year bond is about 20 basis points higher than on a natural 30-year bond, or an extra $2 per bond in interest each year for investors holding the insured issue.

Why does this occur? What is happening here? The two bonds have the same high credit rating, which both of the major rating agencies describe as an absolute standard reserved for the world's most creditworthy institutions. There must be another reason for the yield difference. Is the market simply wrong to grant insured investors the windfall? Or have the rating agencies, in effect, created different levels of Triple-A quality by awarding the rating to some less deserving issues?

We set out to answer those questions and to discover whether economics or perception created the yield differential. We found that the natural Triple-A standard is a very high one indeed, and that Triple-A bonds clearly deserve the rating. More to the yield point, insured Triple-A bonds emerged as stronger than natural Triple-A's for two reasons. First, the insured issue itself is very creditworthy. And second, the addition of the insurer's capital gives the investor another level of protection.

Early in 1992, we began our research, developing our analysis and conclusions during that year. We launched our study by examining yield histories and the factors known to determine yields. Almost without exception, yield factors relate to a bond's default risk and its marketability—how easy it is to sell. Both traits are a matter of investor perception (but are ultimately rooted in economic reality).

We focused next on municipal bond default history and the growth of bond insurance. We also investigated the world of Triple-A bonds.

Natural Triple-A issuers, we found, are mostly thriving cities and states with healthy, diversified economies. But they also include 11 well-endowed colleges and universities, among them Harvard, Yale, Stanford, Notre Dame, and the University of Chicago. These naturals were predominantly general obligation and tax-backed bonds, representing about 6 percent of year-end 1991's $900 billion—or $54 billion—in state and local government debt outstanding.

Insured bonds span a broader field, reflecting the locations and bond types of the overall municipal market. In dollar volume, insured issues account for about 34 percent of the entire municipal market, which was $235 billion at year-end 1992

THE CREDIT RATING PROCESS

In the next phase of our research, we examined the process that lends credibility and cachet to both natural and insured Triple-A's—the rating process. Because insured bonds greatly outnumber naturals, one might assume it is easier for an insurer than an issuer to get a Triple-A.

Just the opposite is true. While both major rating agencies insist that an issuer's financial condition, debt, economic and job base, as well as its management, be outstanding, they demand even more when they rate an insurer.

In addition to an insurer's financial condition, the agencies carefully review its management, its surveillance, and its underwriting practices. They also impose prudent risk-taking guidelines on each individual insurer. Then comes the most important and demanding part of the evaluation. The agencies require the insurer to have enough free capital to survive an economic catastrophe akin to the Great Depression. At the same time, the insurer must be able to meet all obligations to bondholders on time and continue in business after the depression.

Although every bond insurer must pass this highly formal and rigorous stress test, no natural Triple-A issue has ever had to undergo these rigors. For this reason alone, we concluded that if getting a Triple-A is easier for either party, it is demonstrably easier for the natural Triple-A. This became our first hard evidence that investor perception, not economic realities, is a major force behind the insured bond's higher yield.

FINANCIAL TRAITS

Encouraging as this was, we needed more proof. So we reviewed the financial characteristics of natural and insured bonds. We postulated that perhaps overwhelming superiority among the natural Triple-A's would justify the yield differential. Indeed, as you might expect, we found that natural Triple-A issuers do generally have low debt, high taxable asset values, and a prosperous population to pay taxes and fees.

Good as the naturals looked, insured bonds were not far behind in financial quality. And, of course, this was true before we even considered the protective power of the bond insurer's financial resources, which would step into the breach and make timely interest and principal payments to holders should the issuer default.

While this financial evidence definitely supported our thesis, we wanted additional evidence to determine unquestionably whether the yield difference between the two Triple-A's was warranted.

STRESS TEST: SIMULATING THE GREAT DEPRESSION

Any bond's ultimate test is surviving a depression or an extreme recession. A bond that can come through a period as devastating as the Great Depression—the worst economic period in U.S. history—is inherently a better bond.

Thanks to research done for my earlier book, *Risk Based Capital Charges for Municipal Bonds* (JAI Press Inc., 1990), we were able to subject a bond portfolio to a simulated Great Depression and identify bonds likely to default.

Natural Triple-A colleges and universities easily passed the Great Depression test without a single default in our study. However, among tax-backed and general obligation natural Triple-A bonds, defaults equaled 2.6 percent of the average annual debt service. Still, a good record for the Great Depression when nearly 5,000 municipal bonds defaulted.

Among insured bonds, we found that tax-backed and general obligation bonds had a 3.2 percent default rate, while the rate for the total portfolio of insured bonds was 14.6 percent. At first glance, that latter figure appears severe. But not when you look at the whole picture. We must remember that the insurers guaranteeing these bonds also have an asset portfolio they can liquidate to pay bondholders when insured issuers default. Indeed, when we checked the assets of the scenario's insurer (Municipal Bond Investors Assurance Corporation), they were more than adequate to pay all defaults and to keep the company solvent and operating until better economic conditions returned, when the depression period ended.

The scenario's bottom line is that investors in insured bonds benefited tremendously from the double protection provided by the issuer and the insurer. On the contrary, buyers of natural Triple-A bonds did not enjoy this "belt and suspenders" protection, and they lost principal and interest.

Now we had solid proof that insured bonds give better protection against defaults, but this was only half the proof needed to determine which was the better bond.

MARKETABILITY

Marketability is the other half.

Investors regard a bond as marketable when they believe they could sell it easily. We found that the naturals and the insured bonds had advantages and disadvantages in this regard. However, the extra yield that insured bondholders receive over the life of their bond more than offsets its disadvantages. Moreover, marketability, credit quality, and default risk cannot be neatly separated. They are interdependent, and the so-called yield penalty on insured bonds was too steep to be attributed to sales factors alone.

LEARNING FROM OTHER BOND MARKETS

To get a perspective on municipal bond activity, we looked at the government bond market. Here, too, all the issuers are Triple-A, yet yields vary widely. When we adjusted for such technical factors as state and local taxes, we found an amazing collection of misperceptions and little appreciation for inherent bond strength.

We also discovered a classic case of how information can amend perceptions when we compared the Resolution Funding Corporation

(REFCORP), the agency chartered to handle the savings and loan bailout, to a comparable U.S. Treasury bond issued at about the same time.

When REFCORP bonds came to market in October 1989, they yielded 27 basis points, or $2.70 more per bond each year, than the comparable Treasury rate. While REFCORP bonds had essentially the same maturity and exactly the same interest rate, their yield was much greater than Treasuries. On that evidence, you might assume a difference in credit quality.

But, of course, that is not the case. The REFCORP issue is essentially backed by the full faith and credit of the U.S. government, just like Treasuries. The U.S. Treasury will pay REFCORP interest on time if REFCORP cannot. Also, Resolution Funding had to deposit U.S. Treasury Strips with the Federal Reserve bank in an amount equal to the bond's principal at maturity.

Despite this federal backing, REFCORP and Treasury bond yields differed widely on the day REFCORP was sold. Eventually, however, the market began to evaluate the bond more critically, and favorable stories about the issue began appearing in the financial press. Gradually, the yield spread narrowed to 5 to 10 basis points, 50 cents to one dollar per bond each year. Though still not justified, the spread is much narrower than it was on REFCORP's sale day.

From our review of the government bond market, we learned that though bad information and misperceptions are common in the bond market, they can be—and most often are—largely overcome through education and a presentation of the facts.

CONCLUSION

From the evidence we marshaled, it became inescapably clear that investor perception, or, as we believe, misperception, rather than economic reality, is the reason insured municipal bonds generate higher yields than natural Triple-A's. And, no doubt, the windfall insured investors have reaped has increased the popularity of insured bonds. More than likely, the yield gap will close as word of this built-in advantage continues to spread, and as markets become more efficient. Nonetheless, even new investors will still benefit from the added protection that insured bonds offer, and astute initial buyers will be rewarded with capital gains.

CHAPTER 1

PERCEPTION OR REALITY

One of the financial world's most exclusive clubs is the universe of bond issuers that have received a Triple-A credit rating from the two major rating agencies, Moody's Investors Service, Inc. and Standard & Poor's Corporation. These supreme ratings are difficult to earn, easy to lose, and require constant care. And with good reason. Once the coveted Triple-A is lost, it is rarely regained. Moody's and S&P reserve their ratings for the strongest, most creditworthy governments and institutions.

Triple-A ratings are absolute. They have no gradations or shadings of quality such as the pluses or minuses that S&P uses with its other ratings and the numerical subscripts that Moody's employs with its other ratings.

Moody's Bond Record described the bonds that earn Moody's Aaa rating:

> Bonds which are Aaa are generally the best quality. They carry the smallest degree of investment risk and are generally referred to as "gilt edge." Interest payments are protected by a large or by an exceptionally stable margin and principal is secure. While the various protective elements are likely to change, such changes as can be visualized are most unlikely to impair the fundamentally strong position of such issues.

Similarly, S&P's *Municipal Bond Book* characterizes the issues that earn Standard & Poor's AAA: "Debt rated 'AAA' has the highest rating assigned by Standard & Poor's. Capacity to pay interest and repay principal is extremely strong."

The Triple-A is an absolute standard. No issues can be slightly Triple-A or better than other Triple-A's. Moody's *Municipal Issues* underscores the point:

> Moody's is often asked to contrast various Aaa ratings because there are clear trading distinctions and market preferences among the several types of

> Aaa-rated debt. Credits that receive Aaa on their own merits tend to pay a lower rate of interest than insured, Letter of Credit, or securitized Aaa ratings. Some market experts attribute these differentials to the relative scarcity of issues rated Aaa on their own.
>
> Although these trading differentials are not directly Moody's concern, we want to make it very clear that we see no credit distinction among the various issues rated Aaa. Aaa is a measure of absolute quality. When an Aaa rating is assigned the standards for Moody's inclusion are uniformly rigorous. All Aaa-rated bonds offer investors outstanding protection.

Because Triple-A ratings are reserved for the strongest institutions, borrowers with this rating enjoy significant financial advantages. Most important, they can borrow at a lower interest rate because their high-grade debt is less risky and they have greater market access because investors are always seeking high quality bonds.

While the Triple-A is an absolute standard to the rating agencies that bestow it, investors see it differently. In fact, not all Triple-A debt issues are treated equally, as Moody's *Municipal Issues* pointed out. Consistently, issues of comparable maturity and structure trade at different interest rates. This is especially apparent in the municipal bond market. There, Triple-A issues have earned the rating in one of three ways.

So-called natural Triple-A bonds are issued by institutions that have gained the highest rating because of their own financial strength and other protective elements. Enhanced Triple-A bonds get a Triple-A rating because a third party, usually an insurer or a bank issuing a letter of credit, guarantees the timely payment of interest and principal should the investment-grade issuer fail to make the payment. Finally, refunded Triple-A bonds earn the highest rating because enough U.S. Treasury obligations have been placed in escrow to meet all remaining interest and principal payments.

In our examination of municipal bonds rated Triple-A by Moody's and Standard & Poor's, we sought to explain the interest rate differences that exist between natural and insured bonds. We studied the history of the interest rate difference and all literature on differing rates for similar quality bonds. We also reviewed and analyzed many details and intricacies of the Triple-A bond, including its historical performance, market statistics, and other traits.

Since it is central to our study, we described and analyzed the Triple-A rating process for natural and insured issues. And because yield difference almost always results from perceptions of default risk and marketability, we assessed financial and trading attributes of natural and insured bonds. Finally, we examined rate differences in other bond markets for the perspective it might give us on the municipal market.

Our basic purpose was to determine whether the varying interest rates of Triple-A bonds result from rational economic factors or investor misperceptions.

CHAPTER 2

BACKGROUND

At the end of 1991, tax-exempt debt accounted for $1.08 trillion of the total U.S. debt of $14.2 trillion. Tax-exempt debt included $873.2 billion issued by state and local governments, $114 billion by nonfinancial corporate businesses (mostly industrial development and pollution control revenue issues), and $94.9 billion by nonprofit organizations, such as hospitals and private colleges.[1] In this study we will review and analyze only the bonds of state and local governments and nonprofit organizations because their credit nature and general public-purpose funding are similar. We excluded the corporate-backed sector because rather than being traditional municipal bonds, these are corporate issues which are allowed to use tax-exempt financing due to special tax-code provisions. Moreover, they are generally private-activity securities supported by business revenues, not state and local taxes, or relatively essential user fees, as in the case of schools and hospitals.

There are 83,236 state and local government units in the U.S. and about 8,200 nonprofit organizations[2] that can issue tax-exempt debt.

Of these more than 91,000 issuers, only 57 have natural Triple-A ratings from Standard & Poor's and only 126 from Moody's. The 141 issuers with one or more Triple-A ratings have debt outstanding of $58 billion, accounting for 6 percent of the $968.1 billion of state and local and nonprofit, tax-exempt debt outstanding. Insured Triple-A, tax-exempt debt added about $185 billion of par value to the natural Triple-A total. Insured debt on its own comprised 19 percent of the $968.1 billion,[3] which in itself is something of an accomplishment since the bond insurance industry is only slightly more than 20 years old. Bonds were first insured in the early 1970s by AMBAC Indemnity and the Municipal Bond Insurance Association (MBIA). In 1981, only 5 percent of bonds were insured. By 1992, 34 percent of the long-term, new-issue market was guaranteed, primarily by the five Triple-A-rated bond insurance companies.

YIELD HISTORY

Clearly, insured bonds are the largest group of tax-exempt Triple-A's. Yet, a significant yield differential exists between the natural and the insured, as shown in Figure 2–1. In the 1987–92 period, this differential was greatest in 1987 and early 1988. During that period of higher interest rates, the average monthly spread between natural and insured Triple-A's fluctuated between 40 and 80 basis points, $4 to $8 per $1,000 bond per year in additional interest. From 1989 to 1991, the spread averaged 25 to 30 basis points, falling slightly in 1992.

All yield percentages shown are comparable numbers for each of the categories. The discrepancies are not attributable to factors such as tax-rate differentials or geographic location, as both should be common to all yield graphs. Later, we will see that enhanced bonds include several types while most natural Triple-A's are full faith and credit issues backed by taxing power plus several well-endowed universities. As we shall demonstrate, even a spread of 20 basis points between naturals and insureds (a conservative average in recent years) appears unjustified by risk. More likely, this spread results from skepticism or a misunderstanding of the value of such credit enhancement as bond insurance. To begin to explain the differential, we reviewed previous research on the subject.

PREVIOUS LITERATURE

No study has yet explained why bonds enhanced by insurance trade differently than natural Triple-A's. However, some financial analysts have examined the interest-rate spreads of comparable corporate and municipal bonds, and a 1987 paper studied bond insurance's success at lowering the issuer's interest costs. Let's look briefly at five studies.

- In "Statistical Credit Scoring of Municipal Bonds," Willard T. Carleton and Eugene M. Lerner tried to devise a scoring system and test its accuracy for probable Moody's ratings of unrated municipal bonds. At the time, much municipal debt was unrated and Moody's was the major agency rating municipal bonds. Thus, an analytical system of scoring and rating the unrated bonds could make the market more efficient while providing another tool for determining quality and values. How widely the Carleton/Lerner

FIGURE 2–1
Monthly Average Yields—Natural Triple-A versus Insured Triple-A (January 1987–December 1992)

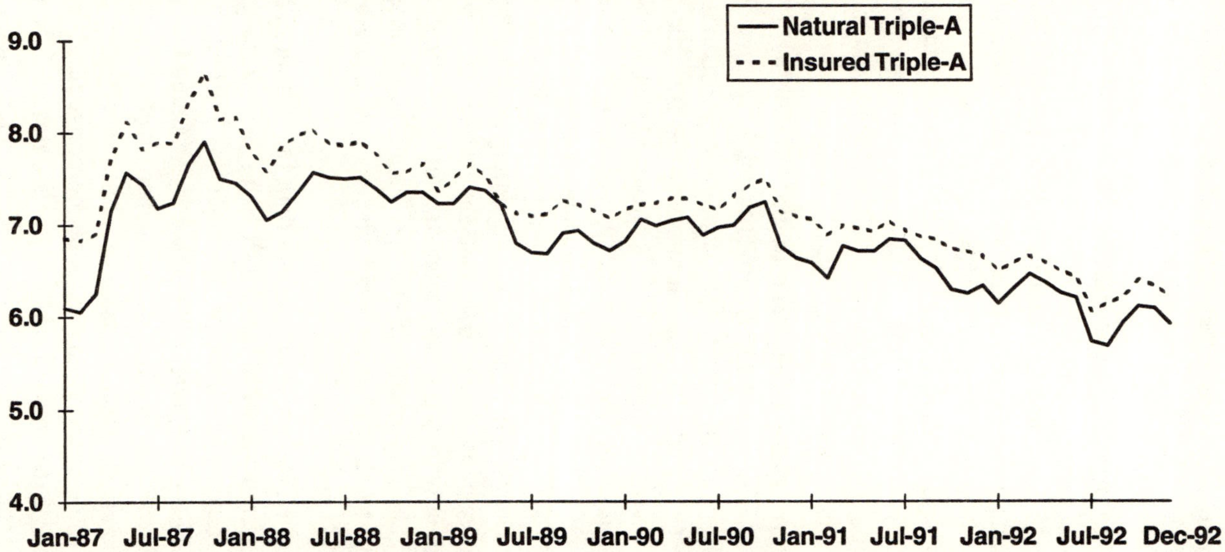

Sources: Natural Triple-A—*Moody's Municipal and Government Manual* and *Moody's Bond Record*. Insured Triple-A—Smith Barney Credit Market Comment. See table in Appendix for yield and spread values.

system, published in the *Journal of Money and Banking*, was used is not known. However, Moody's significantly increased the number of issues it rates, and, since 1969, Standard & Poor's has become a major rater of municipal bonds, adding further efficiency to the market.

Carleton and Lerner's study provides early documentation of the importance of ratings in bond valuation and how information gaps—in this instance, credit ratings—could lead to different values for similar bonds. The authors believed that by studying market inconsistencies caused by an information void and by developing a system to provide ratings, they could make the markets more efficient for bonds of comparable quality.

- Roy W. Bahl, in his 1971 article, "Measuring the Creditworthiness of State and Local Government Municipal Bond Ratings," analyzed rating agency approaches to credit scoring from the bond issuer's perspective. Bahl, stressing the importance of bond ratings, says in the *National Tax Journal* that the wise issuer will look at its official statement (prospectus) from the rating agency perspective and see that the document emphasizes the elements of credit strength that the agency regards as important. In this way, the issuer has the best chance of getting a higher rating and paying a lower interest rate. Bahl also suggests that city governments rethink how they present credit strength to the market; not doing so could be very costly. In essence, Bahl focused on perception in an effort to narrow interest-rate spreads and create a more efficient market.
- Larry Hastie provides an important foundation in his 1972 article "Determinants of Municipal Bond Yields" by analyzing the factors that determine municipal bond yields. Writing in the *Journal of Finance and Quantitative Analysis*, he found two key factors: default risk and marketability, the perceived ease of selling a block of bonds. Thirteen years earlier, Lawrence Fisher made essentially the same observations about the corporate bond market in a 1959 issue of the *Journal of Political Economics*. These two concepts have stood the test of time and are often cited by bond market professionals explaining interest-rate differentials.
- Robert L. Bland and Chilik Yu came very close to some of our investigation's key topics in their 1987 article, "Municipal Bond

Insurance: An Assessment of its Effectiveness at Lowering Costs," which appeared in *Government Finance Review*. To examine the effectiveness of bond insurance, Bland and Yu asked three questions: How do investors value insured bonds? What savings should an issuer expect in interest rates? Is all private bond insurance equally effective at lowering interest costs?

Using 1985 data, Bland and Yu showed that the market did indeed differentiate among insurers. It preferred insurers with two Triple-A ratings—which saved issuers about 14 basis points in interest—over those with only one Triple-A rating from Standard & Poor's. Bland and Yu also found that insured Triple-A bonds tend to trade at interest rates more like those of an uninsured A-rated issuer. They also concluded that the interest cost savings sometimes do not justify the purchase of bond insurance, and it was only effective, in their view, for BBB or Baa-rated issues.

This study identified the value of two Triple-A ratings for bond insurers. When one of today's five major insurers recently had just a single Triple-A rating, its share of the market was less than 3 percent. Essentially, dual Triple-A ratings are *de rigueur* in today's market.

In addition, Bland and Yu's suggestion that issuers should expect bond insurance to produce an interest savings was valid then and more so today. No doubt, in 1985, some bond insurance failed to generate interest savings or generated savings that were imperceptible. In that year, municipal new-issue volume more than doubled over 1984, largely because issuers wanted to get to market ahead of the Tax Reform Act of 1986. This surge in volume created a backlog, preventing the credit rating agencies from rating issues fast enough to get into the market. As a result, the bond insurers functioned as *de facto* rating agencies. When they conferred their Triple-A ratings on an issue, it could readily be sold in the market.

Further using 1985 MBIA data, we examined the relationship between the bond insurance premium and the interest-rate spread. We found that premiums equaled 30 percent of the spread between insured and uninsured interest costs. On average, 70 percent of the savings went to the issuer. In contrast, 1991 premiums on insured issues accounted for only 24 percent of the interest savings, with the balance of 76 percent going to the issuer as savings. Clearly, these data reflect the maturing of the bond insurance industry and the effects of competition.

What level of credit rating benefits most from bond insurance? Using their 1985 data, Bland and Yu concluded that BBB or Baa-rated issues gained the most.

In Table 2–1 we see MBIA's portfolio measured by Moody's rating from 1984 through 1991, by percent of par insured compared to the uninsured market.

Since 1985's high-water mark for its unusually large number of unrated issues, MBIA has insured many more issues rated A or higher, which suggests a more positive perception of bond insurance. That understanding is even clearer when we examine the uninsured market's rating distribution over the same period. Fifty-three percent of the uninsured deals were rated A or higher. In 1986, it dropped to 35 percent and remained at 36 percent in 1991, as insurers increased their share of this market. This improving perception allowed bond insurers to add interest savings in the higher-rated sectors. The Baa sector, at least at MBIA, peaked out in 1986 and in 1987 by par and by number of issues. As the value of insurance has increased, the mix of issues has advanced to higher-quality issues, as one would expect.

Bland and Yu's greatest contributions are their attempt to discover whether the market sees a difference in the value of one bond insurer over another, and their attempt to create a benchmark to measure those differences. Competition and maturity have brought about a more efficient insured municipal bond market as well as a growing appreciation of bond insurance.

TABLE 2–1
Distribution of Moody's Ratings (Percent of Par)

	A or Higher		*Baa or Lower*		*Not Rated*	
	MBIA	*Uninsured*	*MBIA*	*Uninsured*	*MBIA*	*Uninsured*
1984	32	58	4	24	64	19
1985	20	69	4	7	76	24
1986	25	65	12	9	63	26
1991	41	68	10	9	49	23

Source: Uninsured Market: Securities Data Co.

- In his "Analyzing Municipal Quality Spreads," R. B. Davidson, III, quantitatively documents the inefficiency in municipal yields, as well as the overcompensation for default exposure among investment grade municipal bonds. Davidson reviewed the spreads between the rating categories along with municipal bond default history. He concluded that investors who buy and hold A-rated and Baa/BBB-rated bonds are more than adequately compensated for the risk they assume in purchasing lower-grade bonds. Davidson devises a formula for approximating the implied default rates in the spread. He compares this information with historical data and concludes that spreads overly compensate for default risk. If Davidson's premise holds true that investors are amply rewarded by investing in lower-rated bonds because they include no significant defaults, then the investor in insured bonds is well rewarded compared to the investor in natural Triple-A's.

In summarizing the literature, as well as yield histories, two key factors emerge:

- Inconsistent spread relationships exist throughout the spectrum of municipal bond yields, including the Triple-A category.
- These inefficiencies appear rooted in perceptions of default risk and the ability to freely trade issued bonds. No other key causes have been found.

We are going to examine default risk and marketability to determine whether these concerns are based on economic fact or investor perceptions. First, we will review the overall default risk of municipal bonds. Later, we will study insured and natural Triple-A bonds separately to determine their relative risks. We will also examine the credit-rating process to see both natural and insured Triple-A bonds undergo the scrutiny.

MUNICIPAL BOND DEFAULT HISTORY

During the two-century history of municipal bonds in the U.S. capital markets, their credit performance has been exemplary. As we will later demonstrate in detail, much of the default risk investors are compensated for is more perceived than real. First, let us review the overall market statistics.

A brief review of key default data puts the reality of default into perspective. Let's look at bond defaults from 1869 to 1991, which includes the four depressions and eight recessions that occurred since the Civil War.[4] From 1869 to 1991, 7,375 individual bonds have defaulted. Of this total, 5,700, or 77 percent, occurred in the 12 recessions or depressions; 4,782, or 65 percent, occurred during the Great Depression of 1929–38 alone. Only 1,675 defaults, or 23 percent, occurred in relatively normal economic climates[5] (see Figure 2–2).

According to *Bond Buyer* statistics, 614,939 new municipal bond issues came to market from 1896 to 1991. In that same period, 7,012 municipal bonds defaulted, or only 1.1 percent of the issues floated during almost a century.

While some defaults will occur in any period, the greatest credit risk for municipal bonds comes with the type of intense nationwide economic distress that has been largely avoided since the Great Depression. Between 1939 and 1991, only 1,721 defaults occurred, or 23 percent of the total. (See data table in the Appendix.) If one believes the Great Depression was a one-time phenomenon and that reforms now will preclude serious downturns, then the interest-rate premium built into municipal bond yields seems to more than adequately compensate the holder for default risk.

Default data also tend to overstate the risk involved in original issue, investment grade public purpose bonds. Risk is particularly overstated in more modern times thanks to Depression-era reforms and to improved methods introduced since the late 1920s by the rating agencies. Obviously, the rating agencies were more generous in awarding the Triple-A rating before the Depression. A sample of 1929 ratings examined by George Hempel in his 1971 book, *The Post War Quality of State and Local Debt*, showed that 53 percent of rated issues were Triple-A's. In another segment of 264 bonds defaulted during the Depression, 48 percent were rated Triple-A, accounting for 79 percent of the par, according to Hempel. Further, in 1928 all 11 bonds in *The Bond Buyer*'s 11-Bond Index were rated Aaa by Moody's and all were downgraded to Aa or A by 1934.

However, Davidson says that since 1980 only 36 percent of the defaulting amounts in dollars were investment grade at issue. That's roughly $3.2 billion of the $8.9 billion of defaults from 1980 through third-quarter 1990. Sixty-seven percent of the $3.2 billion was Washington Public Power Supply System (WPPSS), a public-purpose issue. In-

FIGURE 2–2
Municipal Bond Defaults and Business Cycle

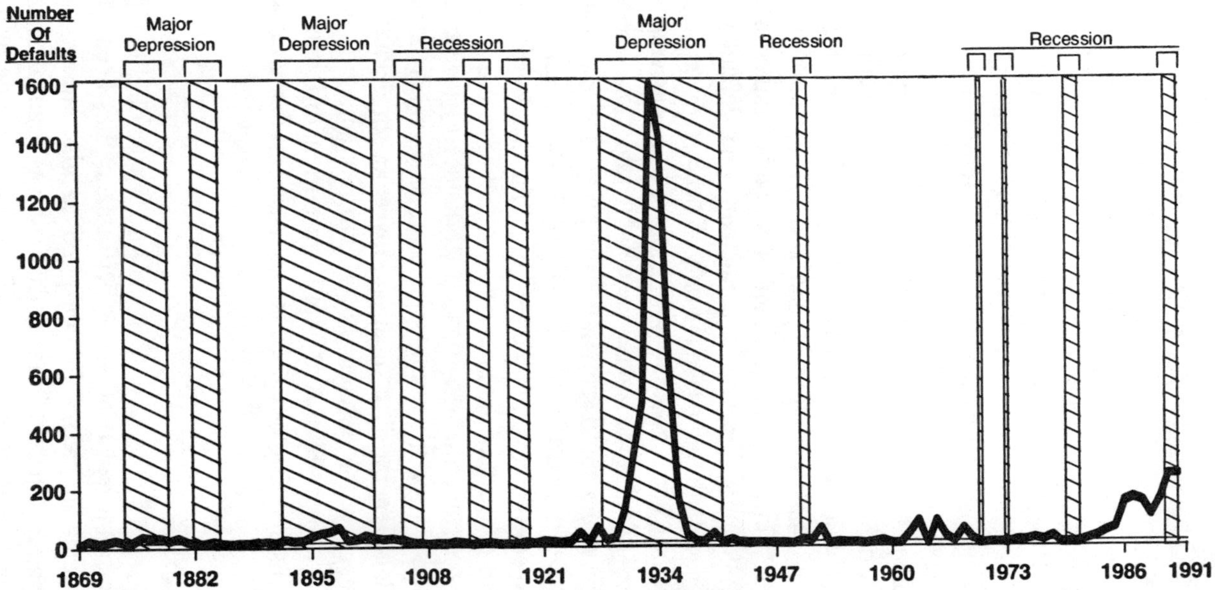

Source: *Risk Based Capital Charges for Municipal Bonds;* Bond Investors Association.

dustrial development bonds, which are not public-purpose issues, accounted for 22 percent of the original investment grade defaults. The remaining 64 percent of defaulting issues began as noninvestment grade and nonpublic purpose. For the most part, they consisted of real estate development, retirement and nursing home, and other industrial revenue bond issues that used tax-exempt conduits for financing purposes. Davidson found no general obligation *bond* defaults since World War II, although some note issues—notably New York City—did default.

Looking at Davidson's statistics in another way, the $8.9 billion of municipal defaults in the 1980–90 period is an average default rate of 0.14 percent of the par value outstanding. In contrast, the high-yield corporate bond market of 1978–90 had an average default rate of almost 2.8 percent, 20 times greater than municipal bonds. And even in 1983, when the WPPSS loss—the largest municipal bond default in history—occurred, the default rate peaked at only .5 percent. Even discounting arguments about what is a public purpose or a true municipal bond, and including all bonds, the aggregate default rate since 1896 of only 1.1 percent by item count is certainly exemplary. The less than 1 percent of the par value over the last decade also underscores truly admirable credit performance. Moreover, 64 percent of all the last decade's defaults never were rated investment grade, a strong signal of future credit problems.

We conclude that the sound performance of investment grade municipal bonds since the Great Depression underscores the point that yield differentials generously compensate investors for default risk. Within a rating category, the difference in default risk among finer gradations is probably imperceptible. And finally, the current differential between natural and insured Triple-A bonds is not based on default risk.

INSURANCE

Although municipal bond credit performance has been very good, two developments in the 1970s conspired to give the insurance industry broader entree to public finance. The first was strained budgets and financial crises that marked major U.S. cities, particularly New York and Cleveland. The second stimulus was created by the shift in municipal bond ownership from institutions to individuals.

Today, municipal bond insurance is the fastest growing segment of the municipal industry. Bond insurance enhances municipal debt by raising the issue's credit rating to Triple-A. Insurance enables the borrower to reduce its interest cost while providing bondholders an additional layer of security through an irrevocable guarantee of timely principal and interest payments for the life of the bond. As economic conditions have fluctuated over the last two decades, the role of bond insurance has steadily increased in the marketplace.

Although bond insurance originated in the late 19th century, the modern practice had to overcome its own obstacles. One of the first positive steps was the Internal Revenue Service ruling that though an insurance company might pay interest on a defaulted tax-exempt bond, the bond would remain tax-exempt. Traders and investors were wary of a product that enhanced one of the safest investments available and reduced its yield. Many issuers also felt enhancement connoted poor credit quality or a failure to access the market.

In the year of AMBAC's founding, Municipal Issuers Service Corporation was established as the managing agency for Municipal Bond Insurance Association (MBIA, now Municipal Bond Investors Assurance Corp.). MBIA insured its first issue in 1974 as a multiline insurer, and Triple-A debt changed in a way that would significantly affect the municipal bond market. MBIA became the first municipal bond insurer to receive a Triple-A rating from any rating agency (in this case, from S&P), its strength derived from the backing of four prominent insurance companies.

During the 1970s, municipal bond insurance activity was sporadic. AMBAC and MBIA each carved a market niche with their AA and AAA ratings, respectively. MBIA remained the sole Triple-A insurance company enhancer of its kind until 1979, when S&P upgraded AMBAC to AAA. However, the financial and economic climate of the early 1980s, plus the tremendous growth in federal debt—which widened spreads—began to broaden opportunities and markets for bond insurers. First, the 20-Bond Index reached a record interest rate of 13.44 percent in January 1982. Days later, Washington Public Power Supply System halted construction on Projects 4 and 5, the prelude to a mammoth municipal bond default. These factors, combined with New York City's 1975 financial problems, seemed to justify the conclusion that municipal obligations were risky.

At the same time, state and local issuers had to cut interest costs; increasingly, they saw the economic value of insurance. Meanwhile, investors began to demand more security for municipal bonds. Of course, these tax-exempt investments were attractive to individual investors in higher tax brackets. Simultaneously, many other tax shelters began to sour or were phased out by tax-code changes. Thus, in the 1980s, individual investors began driving municipal bond insurance by purchasing insured bonds in record numbers, as represented in Figure 2–3. In 1980, they held 30 percent of the outstanding municipal bonds. By 1985, they owned 50 percent, and by 1991, 73 percent.[6] Similar growth occurred in insured bonds. In 1980, 5 percent of the market was guaranteed by insurers. That grew to 21 percent in 1985 and 34 percent in 1992.

Investor demand for insurance prompted other insurance companies to enter the market. Financial Guaranty Insurance Corp. (FGIC) opened its doors in 1983. Another insurance program, Health Industry Bond Insurance (HIBI), created specifically to guarantee health care financings, was launched the same year.

Bond insurance continued to expand as a presence in the market. In 1984, S&P downgraded several major Triple-A U.S. banks, compelling bank letter-of-credit-customers to seek an alternative. About the same time, bond guarantors got a lift when Moody's Investors Service developed a way to rate them. MBIA was granted the first Moody's Aaa rating in July 1984, and FGIC a few months later. By March 1985, two other firms had joined the financial guarantee industry. Bond Investors Guaranty Insurance (BIG) was formed and USF&G added financial guarantees as a product line. Both earned AAA's from S&P just in time to meet the flood of municipal bonds that preceded passage of the Tax Reform Act of 1986.

While Congress debated that legislation, a record $204 billion par value of municipal bonds came to market in 1985. Although bond insurers benefited directly from this huge increase in insurable credits, they also gained indirectly. Issuers often chose to insure their unrated bonds simply to secure an automatic Triple-A, rather than queue up at the overwhelmed rating agencies.

At the same time, the property and casualty insurance industry ran into trouble in its basic business. In September 1985, HIBI, which was underwritten by Industrial Indemnity Insurance Company, a member of the Crum and Forster insurance group, was suspended after insuring $2.7 billion in health and hospital bonds. Industrial Indemnity wanted to "reassess its strategy in financial services and guarantees," reportedly due to cutbacks by Xerox Corp., the parent of Crum and Forster.[7]

The insured Triple-A's reputation was tarnished somewhat in De-

FIGURE 2–3
Individuals as Holders of Total Municipal Debt Outstanding

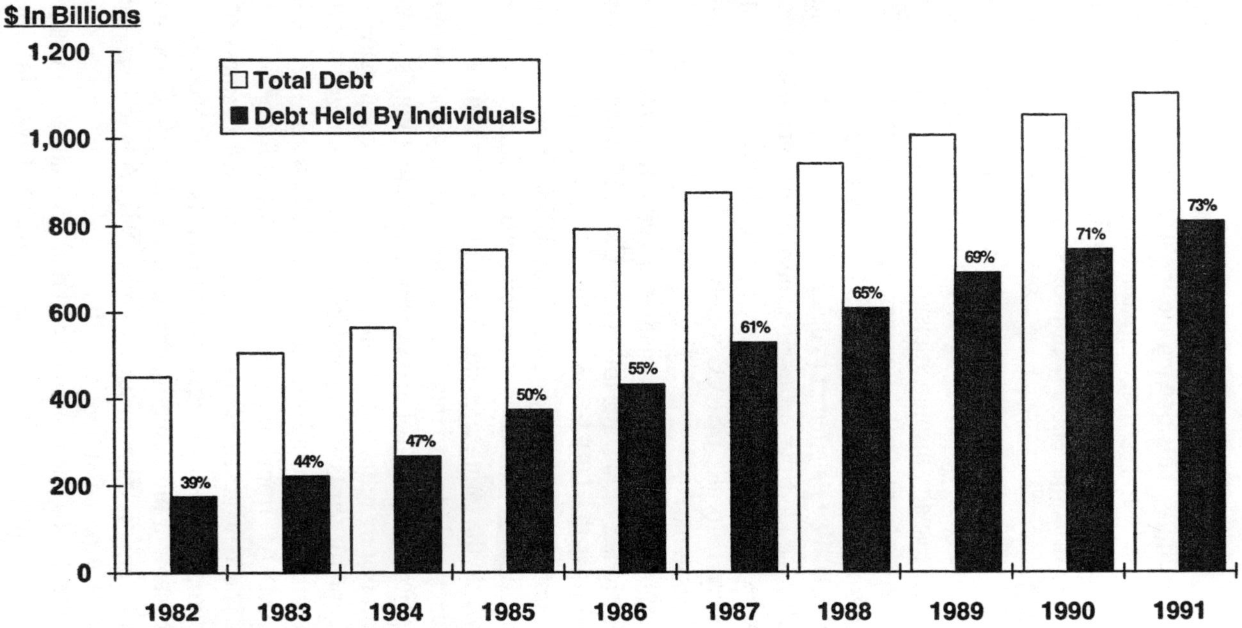

Note: "Individuals" Includes: Households, Mutual Funds, and Money Market Funds.

Source: Federal Reserve Board, *Flow of Fund Accounts, Second Quarter 1992.*

cember 1985 when S&P downgraded to AA all bonds guaranteed by Industrial Indemnity. This downgrade included a number of industrial development bonds and 83 issues guaranteed through HIBI. S&P's action reflected "relatively weak operating and financial performance at Crum and Forster, in conjunction with prospective capital constraints for the company."[8]

Another multiline, US Fidelity and Guaranty Financial Security Co., had been created in March 1985 by the USF&G Corp., the parent of the property and casualty insurer. It insured its first issues in May 1985 with a Triple-A rating from S&P. However, less than a year later, the company lost the rating when S&P downgraded to AA the company's claims-paying ability. USF&G's attempt to diversify had drawn S&P's attention; the agency downgraded the insurer because of its business concentrated in "the riskier casualty lines," not because USF&G was guaranteeing tax-exempt bonds. In all, USF&G's downgrade affected 73 issues totaling $1.1 billion in par.[9]

Bond insurance began to mature in 1986. In September, BIG earned Moody's highest rating. In November, Capital Guaranty Insurance Company assumed the USF&G portfolio and raised the bonds' ratings to AAA. Capital Guaranty was created by USF&G and a group of institutional investors as a monoline financial guarantee company with an S&P rating. While the rating agencies were developing formal models of capital adequacy and ways to monitor the credit quality and composition of an insurer's portfolio, the volume of new tax-exempt bonds returned to normal, and insurers remained strong players in the bond market.

Except for shifts in ownership, no major changes occurred among financial guarantee companies in the mid-1980s. In 1985, Citibank purchased AMBAC from the estate of its bankrupt former owner, Baldwin-United. The new AMBAC assumed the in-force business of the predecessor company and subsequently gained its own Moody's Aaa rating. MBIA became a monoline insurer in December 1986 and made its first public offering of common stock in mid-1987. A year later, General Electric Credit Corporation bought FGIC.

In the 1990s, new municipal bond guarantee companies emerged. Financial Security Assurance (FSA), which began insuring corporate bonds in 1985, added municipal bond insurance in 1990. Connie Lee Insurance Company backed its first higher education bond in the primary market in October 1991. Congress had created the College Construction Loan Insurance Association, as Connie Lee is formally known, in 1986 to provide insurance and reinsurance for educational borrowers in the lower credit quality ranges. In 1991, AMBAC offered its stock to the public.

As bond insurers proliferated and competition intensified, insurance rapidly penetrated the total market. The insured portion went from 18 percent of all new issues in 1987 to 34 percent in 1992 (see Figure 2–5). Seeking security, individual investors drove this demand, and in 1991 they held 73 percent of municipal debt.

FIGURE 2–4
Bond Insurers—Ratings History

1971	February: AMBAC Created -- S&P AA
1973	June: MBIA Created
1974	May: MBIA Issues 1st Policy -- S&P AAA
1979	December: AMBAC Receives S&P AAA
1983	September: FGIC Created -- S&P AA December: FGIC Receives S&P AAA June: HIBI Program Starts S&P AAA
1984	July: MBIA -- Aaa by Moody's October: FGIC -- Aaa by Moody's
1985	March: USF&G -- S&P AAA March: BIG Created -- S&P AAA June: AMBAC -- Aaa by Moody's September: HIBI Suspended December: HIBI Bonds Downgraded to AA by S&P
1986	April: USF&G Downgraded to AA by S&P September: BIG -- Aaa by Moody's November: Capital Guaranty. -- S&P AAA Assumes USF&G Portfolio
1989	December: MBIA Assumes BIG Portfolio
1990	July: FSA Insures First Municipal Bond -- AAA/Aaa
1991	November: Connie Lee Insures First Municipal Bond -- S&P AAA

FIGURE 2–5
New Issue Municipal Bonds (Total Volume versus Insured Percent of Total, 1971–1991)

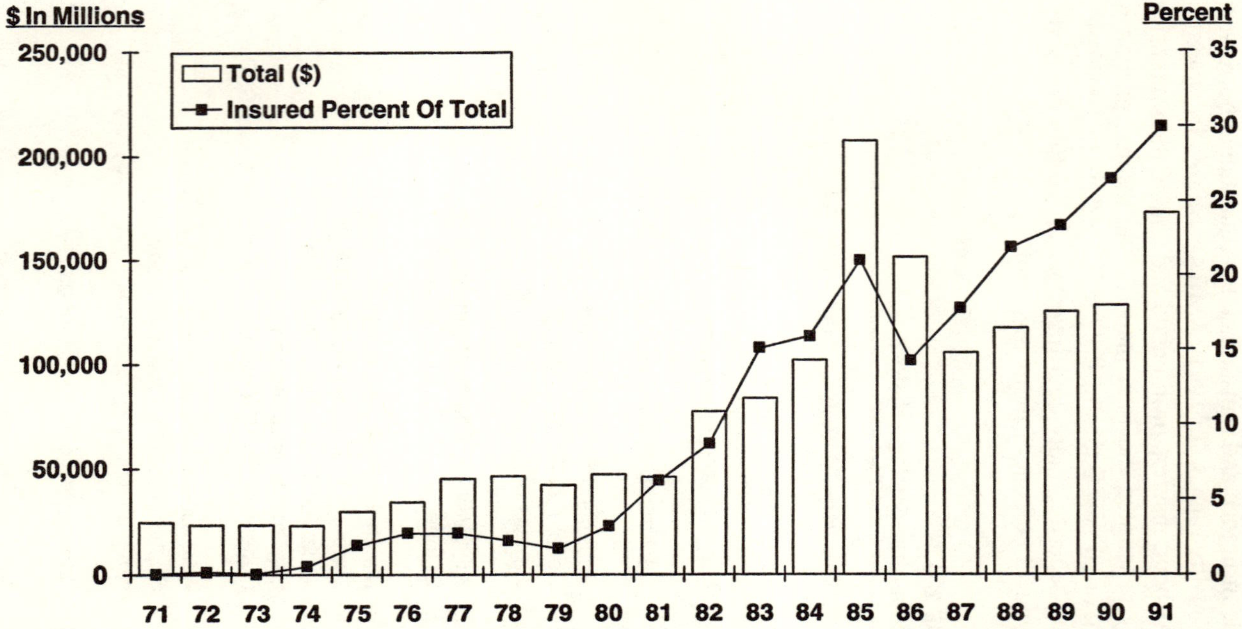

Source: *The Bond Buyer Yearbook*, 1980–1991 editions; MBIA and AMBAC Reports.

In their industry's relatively short history, municipal bond insurers have not had to weather a major depression, but AMBAC and MBIA have coped with three recessions. Each has sustained losses and had major changes in ownership. In the process, each has built its resources and raised market presence to a level few would have imagined only 20 years ago. Late in 1990, S&P commented on the skeptical view that the weakening economy would negatively affect bond insurers.

> In many respects, the (bond insurance) industry is healthier than ever. Net income has reached record levels, statutory capital levels have continued to grow, underwriting quality has been maintained, and losses continue to be incurred at nominal levels. . . . The ability of bond insurers to weather losses without damage to their "AAA" ratings ranges from satisfactory to excellent.[10]

This strength and popularity is very clear in the insured market's 1992 performance. As their core business of insuring municipal issues is now firmly established, insurers are seeking new market opportunities.

Later, we will see that natural Triple-A's do not necessarily stay that way forever. An issuer's ability to retain a Triple-A by insuring a financing is more certain and predictable. Since the industry was formed more than two decades ago, its track record is outstanding; no monoline financial guarantee insurance company has ever been downgraded and no insured bond investor has failed to receive an insured bond payment on time. The spread of this business and its continued adherence to sound underwriting discipline strongly suggest that this method of credit enhancement will maintain its unblemished record.

NOTES

1. Board of Governors of the Federal Reserve System, *Flow of Funds Accounts, Fourth Quarter 1991*, Annual Revisions, Washington, D.C.
2. U.S. Bureau of the Census, *Statistical Abstract of the United States*, 1987, 1989, Washington, D.C.: U.S. Government Printing Office.
3. Association of Financial Guaranty Insurors (AFGI), 1991 Annual Report.
4. As defined by the National Bureau of Economic Research: a depression is three or more consecutive years of contraction in the economy, a major recession is two consecutive years of contraction, and a post–World War II recession is one year of contraction. All periods include leading or following

years where economic history or conventional wisdom labeled the period as a depression or recession.

5. Robert R. Godfrey, *Risk Based Capital Charges for Municipal Bonds* (Greenwich: JAI Press Inc., 1990); and Bond Investors Association.
6. Board of Governors of the Federal Reserve System, *Flow of Funds Accounts, Second Quarter 1992*, Washington, D.C.
7. Joe Mysak, "Bond Insurer Halts Guarantees through Its HIBI Program," *The Bond Buyer*, September 24, 1985, p. 1.
8. Standard & Poor's Corporation, "Ratings Lowered on $5.2 Billion of Insured Debt," *Standard & Poor's Creditweek*, December 23, 1985, p. 10.
9. Standard & Poor's Corporation, "USF&G's Claims-Paying Ability Cut to 'AA'," *Standard & Poor's Creditweek*, April 28, 1986, p. 20.
10. Standard & Poor's Corporation, "Municipal Insurers' Staying Power Debated," *Standard & Poor's Credit Review*, November 26, 1990, p. 3.

CHAPTER 3

TRIPLE-A QUALITY: BORN AND BOUGHT

Bond issues become Triple-A in one of three ways. They are born that way—the natural Triple-A's. They are refunded or escrowed with enough U.S. Treasury obligations to assure payment of outstanding principal and interest. Or, they are enhanced by a third party with a Triple-A rating. We will profile both natural and insured Triple-A's to mark their similarities and differences as we seek clues to their different trading values. We will review their components, history, and market statistics from 1971 to the present, an ample period to study trends, fluctuations, and evolutions among the bonds in each category.

NATURAL TRIPLE-A'S: BORN THAT WAY

A glance at the roster of tax-exempt issuers with natural Triple-A ratings, listed in Table 3–1 reveals several things immediately. All the states are prosperous with diversified economies. The cities, counties, and school districts are in major metropolitan areas surrounded by healthy economies or affluent suburbs. The universities are financially solid, old-line, "household" names. The balance look like revenue bond issues, but most are actually backed by a state or significant local taxing power.

Homogeneity is another group hallmark. Data for 1991 say 94 percent of the par value issued by natural Triple-A credits is tax backed or general obligation while 6 percent is university revenue bonds. Historically, bond investors prefer full faith and credit or general obligation issues while demanding yield premiums for revenue bonds. In addition, to investors, natural Triple-A general obligations have "unlimited taxing power." Thus, one should not be surprised to find the bulk of natural Triple-A's in the general obligation category.

TABLE 3–1
Natural Triple-A Rated Outstanding Debt (Noncorporate Tax-exempt Issuers as of 12/31/91)

Agency	Issuer	
	States	
(M)	California	
(M)	Georgia	
(M) (S)	Maryland	
(M) (S)	Missouri	
(M)	New Jersey	
(M) (S)	North Carolina	
(M) (S)	South Carolina	
(M)	Tennessee	
(M) (S)	Utah	
(M) (S)	Virginia	
	Cities, Towns, and Villages	
(M)	Alexandria	VA
(M)	Belmont Town	MA
(M)	Berkeley Heights Township	NJ
(M)	Cedar Rapids	IA
(M) (S)	Charlotte	NC
(M) (S)	Charlottesville	VA
(M)	Concord Town	MA
(M) (S)	Dallas	TX
(M)	Darien	CT
(M)	Des Moines	IA
(S)	Durham	NC
(M)	Evanston	IL
(M) (S)	Fairfield Town	CT
(M)	Florham Park Borough	NJ
(M)	Germantown	TN
(M)	Glenview	IL
(S)	Greensboro	NC
(M)	Indianapolis	IN
(M)	Iowa City	IA
(M)	Irving	TX
(M)	Kings Point	NY
(M)	Lake Forest	IL
(M)	Lexington	MA
(S)	Lincoln	NE
(M)	Los Angeles	CA
(M) (S)	Lower Merion Township	PA
(M)	Madison	WI
(M)	Millburn Township	NJ
(M) (S)	Minneapolis	MN

TABLE 3–1 (*continued*)

Agency	*Issuer*	
(M)	Minnetonka	MN
(M)	New Canaan	CT
(M)	Newton	MA
(M) (S)	Omaha	NE
(M) (S)	Overland Park	KS
(M)	Palm Beach	FL
(M)	Portland	OR
(M)	Princeton Borough	NJ
(M)	Princeton Township	NJ
(M) (S)	Raleigh	NC
(M) (S)	Rochester	MN
(M)	Rye	NY
(M)	Salt Lake City	UT
(M)	San Diego	CA
(M)	Scarsdale Village	NY
(M) (S)	Stamford	CT
(M)	Summit	NJ
(M)	Wauwatosa	WI
(M)	Wellesley	MA
(M) (S)	West Hartford	CT
(M)	Weston	MA
(M)	Weston	CT
(M)	Westport	CT
(M)	Wilton	CT
(M)	Winchester	MA
(M)	Winnetka	IL
(S)	Winston–Salem	NC
	Counties	
(M) (S)	Arlington	VA
(M)	Baltimore	MD
(M)	Bergen	NJ
(M)	Chesterfield	VA
(M) (S)	Dallas	TX
(M)	Dane	WI
(M) (S)	DuPage	IL
(M) (S)	Durham	NC
(M) (S)	Fairfax	VA
(M)	Franklin	OH
(M)	Hamilton	OH
(M) (S)	Hennepin	MN
(M) (S)	Henrico	VA
(S)	Kent	MI
(M)	Marion	IN
(M) (S)	Mecklenburg	NC

TABLE 3–1 (*continued*)

Agency	*Issuer*	
(M)	Merrimack	NH
(M)	Middlesex	NJ
(M) (S)	Montgomery	MD
(M)	Montgomery	PA
(M) (S)	Morris	NJ
(M)	Ramsey	MN
(M)	Salt Lake	UT
(M) (S)	Somerset	NJ
(M)	Union	NJ
(M) (S)	Wake	NC
(M)	Waukesha	WI
(M) (S)	Westchester	NY
	School Districts	
(M)	Bloomfield Hills SD	MI
(M)	Dallas I.S.D.	TX
(S)	Douglas Co. S.D. #1	NE
(M)	Great Neck Union Free	NY
(M)	Highland Park I.S.D. (Dallas Co.)	TX
(S)	Kent I.S.D.	MI
(M)	Lake Co. S.D. #67	IL
(S)	Lancaster P.S.D. #1	NE
(M) (S)	Lower Merion Twp. S.D.	PA
(M)	Madison Metropolitan S.D.	WI
(M)	Millburn Township S.D.	NJ
(M)	Princeton Regional S.D.	NJ
(M)	Rochester I.S.D. #535	MN
(M)	Scarsdale Union Free S.D.	NY
(M)	Tredyffrin/Easttown S.D.	PA
(M)	Wauwatosa S.D.	WI
	Universities	
(M) (S)	California Educational Facilities Authority California Institute of Technology	CA
(M) (S)	California Educational Facilities Authority Stanford University	CA
(M) (S)	Connecticut Health & Educational Facilities Authority Yale University	CT
(M)	Illinois Educational Facilities Authority University of Chicago	IL
(M)	Indiana Educational Facilities Authority University of Notre Dame	IN
(M) (S)	Massachusetts Health and Educational Facilities Authority Harvard University	MA

TABLE 3–1 (*concluded*)

Agency	*Issuer*	
(M)	Massachusetts Health and Educational Facilities Authority Massachusetts Institute of Technology	MA
(M) (S)	New Jersey Educational Facilities Authority Princeton University	NJ
(M)	New Jersey Educational Facilities Authority Institute for Advanced Studies at Princeton	NJ
(M)	New York State Dormitory Authority Columbia University	NY
(M) (S)	New York State Dormitory Authority Rockefeller University	NY
	Other	
(S)	Arizona Department of Transportation	AZ
(M) (S)	Dallas County Community College District	TX
(M) (S)	Durham & Wake County Special Airport District	NC
(M)	East Bay Municipal Utilities District	CA
(M)	Indianapolis–Marion County Public Library District	IN
(S)	Illinois Sales Tax	IL
(M)	Johnson County Community College District	KS
(S)	Lancaster County Institutional District	PA
(M)	Long Beach Gas	CA
(M)	Los Angeles Flood Control District	CA
(S)	Madison Area Vocational Technical and Adult Education District #4	WI
(M)	Madison Metropolitan Sewer District	WI
(S)	Maryland National Park & Plan Commission	MD
(M)	Metro Water District of Southern California	CA
(M) (S)	Minneapolis–St. Paul Metro Airport Commission	MN
(M) (S)	Minneapolis–St. Paul Metro Council	MN
(S)	Ohio Highway Improvement Bonds	OH
(M)	San Antonio Electric and Gas Revenue	TX
(M)	San Diego County Water Authority	CA
(S)	Springfield Sanitation District	IL

M—Moody's; S—Standard & Poor's

Source: Data from Moody's and Standard & Poor's publications.

How have naturals changed over the last 20 years? At the end of 1971, one or both agencies had rated 151 issuers Triple-A on their own merits. In 1981, it rose to 168, and in 1991 it declined to 141. Although these numbers don't vary greatly over two decades, each agency reports significant variations. In 1971, S&P rated 120 issuers as AAA; Moody's designated 71. By 1991, issuers with Triple-A's totaled 57 by S&P, and 126 by Moody's. Figure 3–1 represents the yearly totals of Triple-A issuers by each agency. In the early 1970s, the yearly totals of Triple-A's by each agency moved in opposite directions. S&P gradually reduced the number of Triple-A's during the decade, while Moody's significantly increased them. Both agencies downgraded many Triple-A's in 1982–83, as the economic recession affected the debt-paying ability of many municipalities. Since then, Triple-A ratings have leveled off.

Another way to describe natural Triple-A's is by their survival rate. Of the 151 Triple-A issuers in 1971, 27 were still outstanding in 1991. The survivors include seven states (among them California and New Jersey, downgraded by Moody's in 1992) and some affluent areas such as New York's Westchester County and Stamford, Connecticut. Going a step further, we can calculate the average life of a natural Triple-A since 1971. For Moody's Triple-A issuers, the average life is 10 years; for S&P issuers, eight years. Once lost, a Triple-A rating is seldom regained. Only six issuers downgraded during our 20-year period were upgraded, and two of these were downgraded again.

A third way to analyze natural Triple-A's is geographically. The municipalities and universities rated Triple-A in 1971 were somewhat more dispersed geographically, representing 32 different states, compared with 25 states in 1991. In 1971, most issuers were located in the Northeastern and North Central states. At the end of 1971, at least one agency rated all of the Northeastern states, Connecticut, Massachusetts, Maine, New Hampshire, New Jersey, New York, and Vermont, Triple-A. None kept its Triple-A for general obligation bonds through 1991 except New Jersey, and Moody's downgraded it in August 1992. The Texas recession in the second half of the 1980s also resulted in many downgrades, particularly the city of Houston and other Harris County credits. Throughout the 20-year span, many of the towns, school districts, and special districts were associated with a major metropolitan area. As local economies were strained over the last decade, Triple-A issuers have become concentrated around the most prosperous cities. Figures 3–2 and 3–3 map the location of Triple-A municipal issuers in 1971 and 1991.

Although the 1991 list includes about as many issuers as the 1971 list, recent trends and actions by the rating agencies have held natural Triple-A issuers to a relatively small number and reaffirmed their vulnerability. In a six-month period in 1991, S&P downgraded the general obligations of California, New Jersey, and Maine from AAA. Only six Triple-A states remain, and South Carolina's AAA general obligation debt was placed on Credit Watch, a credit-alert list, in 1992.

Overall municipal ratings were hit hard by the 1991 recession. S&P downgraded $53.1 billion in debt in 1991; only $8 billion was upgraded.[1] The trend continued in the first half of 1992; $22.7 billion of S&P municipal ratings were lowered, offset by only $13.8 billion in upgrades.[2] At Moody's, the decline was less dramatic. In 1991, $27 billion in total debt was lowered while $23 billion was raised.[3] However, in the first half of 1992, the $35.3 billion in downgrades outpaced the $6.2 billion in upgrades.[4] The vast majority of these downgrades were general obligations. Revenue bonds fare better because they have greater flexibility in meeting debt service payments. They also are less likely to be affected by economic events.

Since 1971, it is clear, the ratings of natural Triple-A's have been affected by regional economic events, politically influenced financial decisions, and other factors. In short, a myriad of variables bear on the strength and resilience of the natural Triple-A, in sharp contrast to the insured Triple-A.

INSURED TRIPLE-A'S: A DIVERSE PORTFOLIO

All types of issuers make up the typical insured portfolio of a financial guarantor. From the start, bond insurance has been used across all traditional types of securities and geographic boundaries. Generally, it is limited by credit factors. An issuer may be rated highly enough so that its bonds trade on their own without a cost benefit to the issuer. Or a bond's creditworthiness may be below an insurer's risk threshold, as measured by its underwriting criteria. Other than internal restrictions or policies, the only limitation is from state insurance departments, which primarily limit an insurer to a single risk, or from the rating agencies, which want to see a strong, investment grade, insured portfolio.

Natural Triple-A debt is fairly homogeneous, with general obligation or related tax-backed securities (i.e., sales tax) accounting for nearly all of it. In 1991, 94 percent of the natural Triple-A rated par issued was tax-backed; in 1990, it was 99.6 percent, and in 1989, 91.5 percent. University revenue bonds made up the balance of the newly issued debt.

In contrast, insured bonds spanned a much wider spectrum in 1991. See Table 3–2.

FIGURE 3–1
Outstanding Natural Triple-A Issuers (1971–1991)

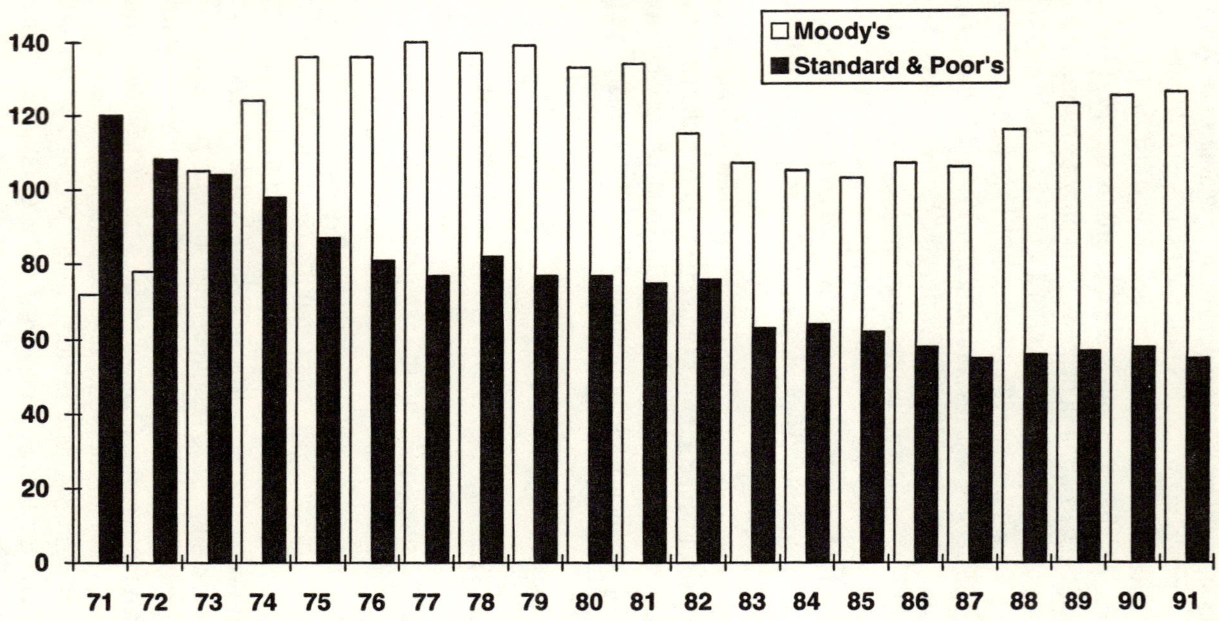

Source: Moody's and Standard & Poor's publications.

FIGURE 3–2
1971 Triple-A Rated States, Counties, and Cities

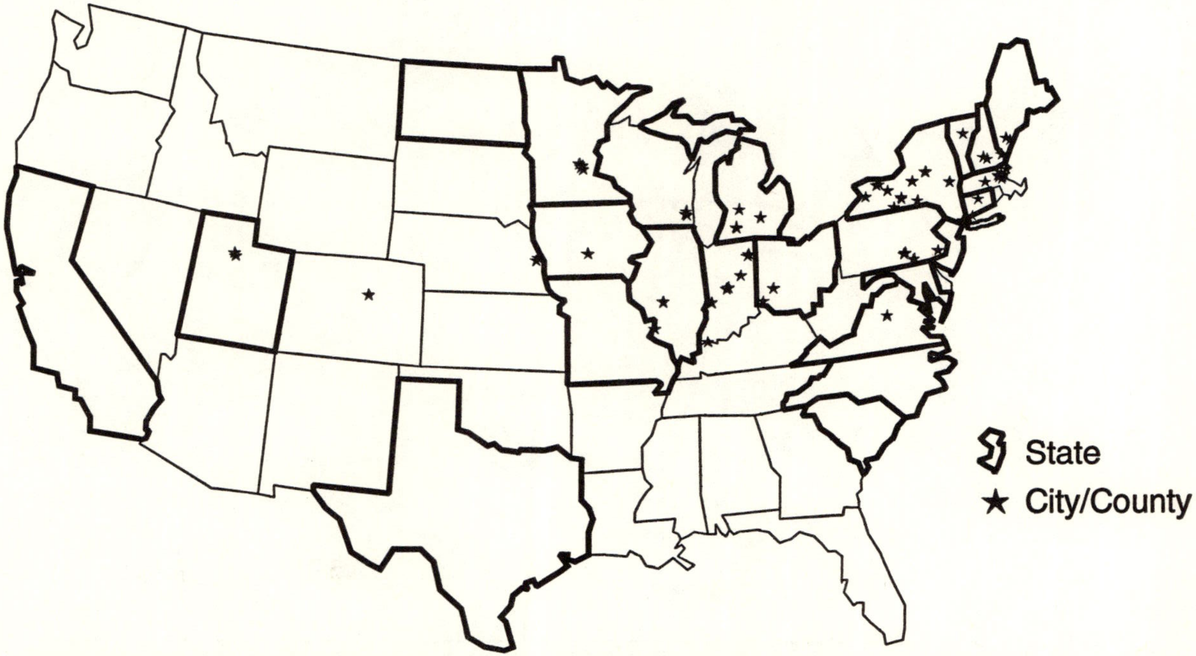

Source: Moody's and Standard & Poor's publications.

FIGURE 3–3
1991 Triple-A Rated States, Counties, and Cities

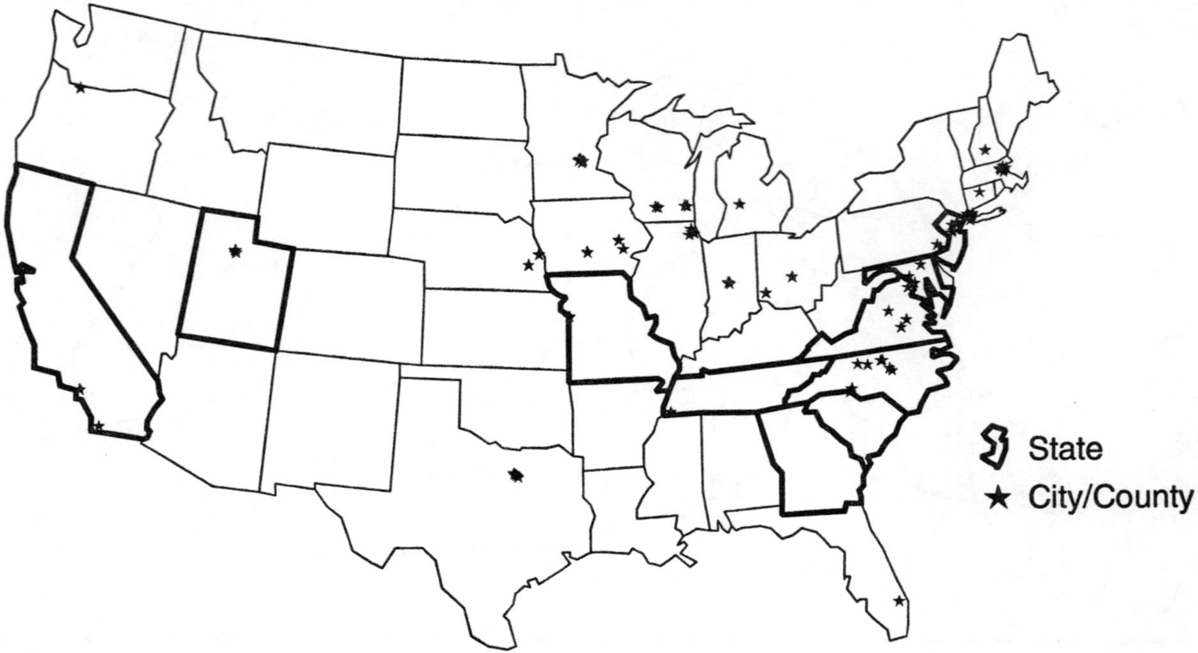

Source: Moody's and Standard & Poor's publications.

TABLE 3–2
1991 Insured Municipal Bond Market Distribution by Type

Bond Type	*Percent of Par Value Insured*
General obligation	36
Utilities (including corporate)	19
Hospitals	13
Colleges and universities	4
Transportation	6
Special revenue	4
Asset backed	15
All other	3
Total	100

Source: AFGI 1991 Annual Report.

Results in recent years have been comparable, and the bond insurers' portfolios have tended to mirror the overall market, which, by bond type, was 34 percent general obligation and 66 percent revenue bonds in 1991.

Bond insurers' portfolios have also been characterized by geographic diversification. Most insurers believe this step protects against geographically linked risks, such as natural disasters and regional economic factors. Bond insurance has been used by issuers in all 50 states, as well as Washington, D.C., Puerto Rico, and Guam. Usage is concentrated among states with high overall issuance that are the more populated, industrialized areas. The top 10 states, measured by total 1991 new issue volume and the portion of par value insured, are summarized in Table 3–3.

MARKET STATISTICS

In relative terms, the group of natural Triple-A's is a small portion of the market, particularly of rated issues. In 1989, 47 percent of Moody's outstanding ratings were Aaa; 70 percent of those were through bond insurance, only 1 percent of those were natural.[5] In 1991, Moody's indicated that 1.5 percent of all general obligation ratings were Aaa on their own.[6] To examine the significance of par value issued among these entities, as well as the frequency and average size of issuance, we compiled the totals of new issue bonds issued by natural Triple-A entities for 1989–91. Only

TABLE 3–3
1991 Municipal Bond New Issuance Volume (Top 10 States; Par in $ Millions)

Rank		*New Issue Total Par Value*		*New Issue Insured Par Value*
1	CA	$24,764	CA	$6,208
2	NY	20,571	PA	6,039
3	TX	11,489	FL	4,993
4	PA	9,793	TX	3,638
5	FL	9,077	NY	3,607
6	NJ	7,531	NJ	2,536
7	IL	6,693	IL	1,960
8	MA	4,806	MI	1,940
9	MI	4,775	OH	1,500
10	WA	4,500	MA	1,189
Total		$103,999		$33,610
Total market all states		$172,576		$51,685
Top 10/Total		60.3%		65.0%

Source: *Bond Buyer 1992 Yearbook;* Securities Data Co.

long-term debt sold by an issuer rated Triple-A by either agency at the time of sale is included.

Overall, the municipal market from 1989 through 1991 demonstrated proportionally more growth in the insured Triple-A for the period, and even more expansion growth in natural Triple-A bonds. Insured Triple-A's comprised 24.8 percent in 1989, and natural Triple-A's were 4.4 percent. In 1991, the insured market had grown to 30 percent, and natural Triple-A par had increased to 6.1 percent of the total (see Figure 3–4).

Although the growth patterns are parallel, the impetus for growth is not. The recent rise in insured bonds reflects concern about greater risk among unsecured financings in a changeable economy. Prime examples are the highly publicized downgrading of Philadelphia and the attempted bankruptcy of Bridgeport, Connecticut. Insurance is also increasingly in demand for revenue bond financings, which are generally viewed as riskier than tax-supported obligations.

The increase in natural Triple-A bonds has different causes. It is propelled by the cities' specific needs, often to take advantage of low interest rates to issue or refinance debt. The par value of state general obligation bonds was easily the most significant, although only 12 states were involved each year. Par issued by these states accounted for 61 percent of the 1989 total, and 68 percent of the 1991 total. California alone is responsible for the bulk of the state-issued bonds, accounting for 30 percent, 45 percent, and 40 percent of all natural Triple-A issuance from 1989 to 1991.

Referring to California's huge debt issuance, Moody's pointed out that, ". . . California has an economy larger than that of most sovereign nations. It is the largest in population and among the most diverse and affluent states."[7] California's growing population prompted the sale of over $8.6 billion in general obligation bonds in the 1989–91 period, directly contributing to the gain in the natural Triple-A market during that time. Infrastructure and education needs have been substantial; the school-age population has grown at almost twice the rate of the state's general population.

In late 1991, the roster of natural Triple-A's lost its dominant player when S&P downgraded California; Moody's followed a month later.

When examining 1989–91 issuance patterns, we immediately see that the average annual amount was related to issuer type. States had by far the highest average size, followed by counties, cities/towns, and school districts. The Triple-A universities and the "other" category were less consistent. Except for most of the states and several of the county issuers, issuers floated less than one issue per year.

Because states dominate the natural category, natural issues tend to be much larger than insured issues, which are usually more indicative of the overall bond market (see Table 3–4).

Geographic distribution is another quantifiable trait of both natural and insured Triple-A's. In 1991, 25 states were represented by issuers rated Triple-A on their own. This was consistent with 1989 and 1990 data. The scope of the insured par distribution is much broader. In each of those years, issues were insured in every state.

Table 3–4
Average Size Comparison of Natural and Insured Issues

	Natural	*Insured*
1989	$56 million	$17 million
1990	$67 million	$18 million
1991	$84 million	$20 million

FIGURE 3–4
Triple-A Issuance versus Market (1989–1991)

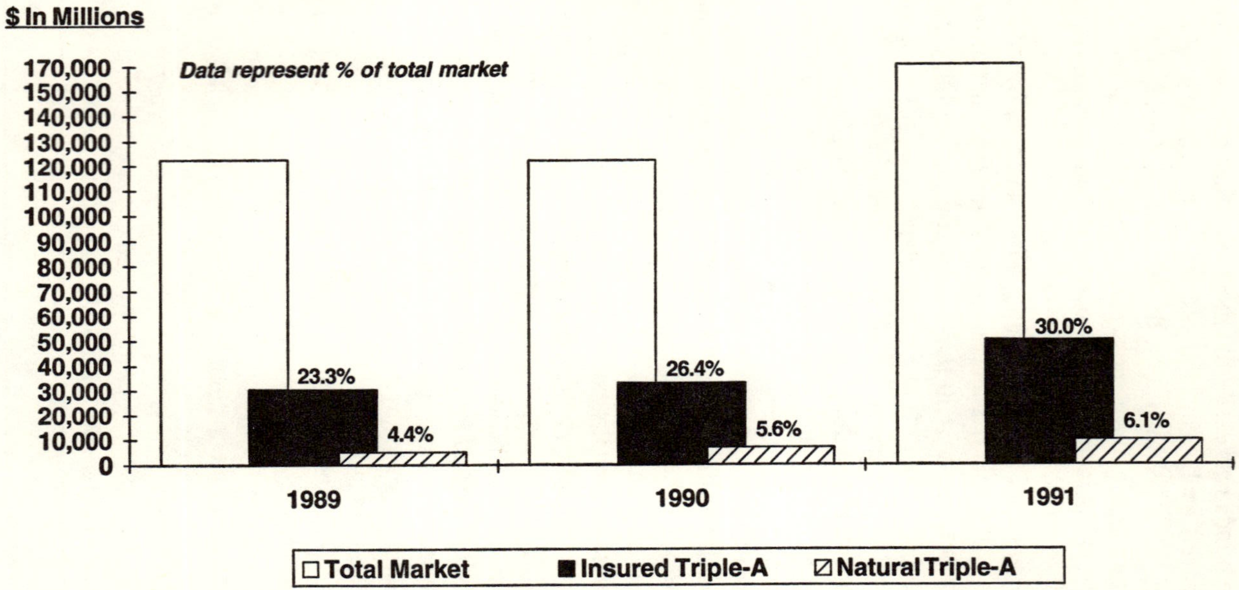

Source: MBIA market data.

During the first half of 1992, the total issuance of natural Triple-A par accounted for only 4.1 percent of the total market, down from the 6.1 percent for all of 1991. The impact of the California downgrade is evident. In the first six months of 1992, state issuers accounted for only 37 percent of the natural Triple-A par, down from 68 percent in 1991. The insured market reached its highest share at 36 percent for the first half of 1992. Recession, quality among municipal credits, and increasing demand for insurance by individual investors contributed to that record share.

CONCLUSIONS

The most striking difference between natural and insured Triple-A bonds is their distribution by bond type. Naturals are predominantly issues backed by prosperous and broad tax bases, plus a few old, well-endowed institutions of higher learning. Insured Triple-A's are a diverse mix more indicative of the total municipal bond market—approximately one-third general obligation and two-thirds revenue bonds. Conventional wisdom perpetuated over the years holds that general obligation bonds are much safer because of the "unlimited" taxing powers, while revenue bonds have limited revenue raising flexibility in a downturn. However, the evolutionary chart of natural Triple-A issuers in Figure 3–5 shows that political reality has repeatedly intervened to dampen the myth of "unlimited" taxing power. California, with the most diverse, and until recently, one of the most prosperous economies in the U.S. (perhaps in the world), could not summon the forces necessary to retain its Triple-A rating. Moreover, revenue bonds today in many instances may be better secured and more likely to avoid default than their general obligation counterparts. In a later chapter, we will review the key financial attributes of the two bond groups in more detail to determine relative actual strength. Before doing so, however, we need to analyze the rating process of Moody's and S&P to see if the agencies award them the Triple-A in fundamentally different ways.

NOTES

1. Standard & Poor's Corporation, "Municipal Ratings Hit Hard," *Standard & Poor's Credit Review*, February 3, 1992, pp 28–29

FIGURE 3–5

A. Moody's Outstanding Natural Triple-A Issuers (1971–1991)

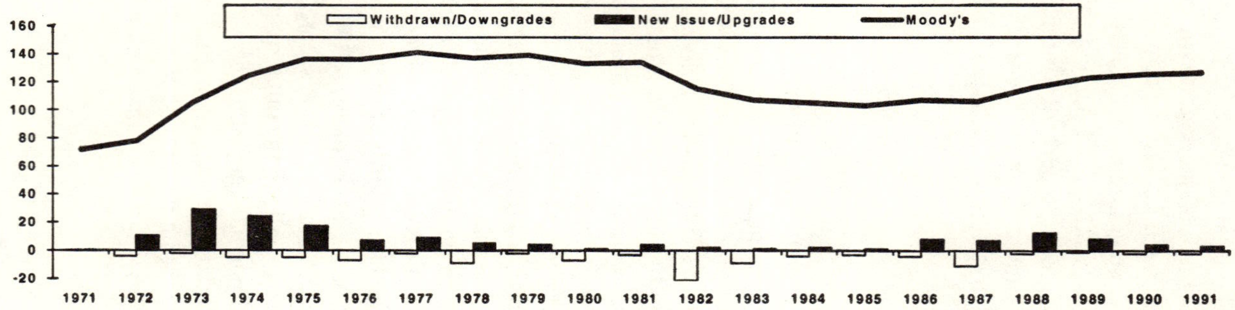

B. Standard & Poor's Outstanding Natural Triple-A Issuers (1971–1991)

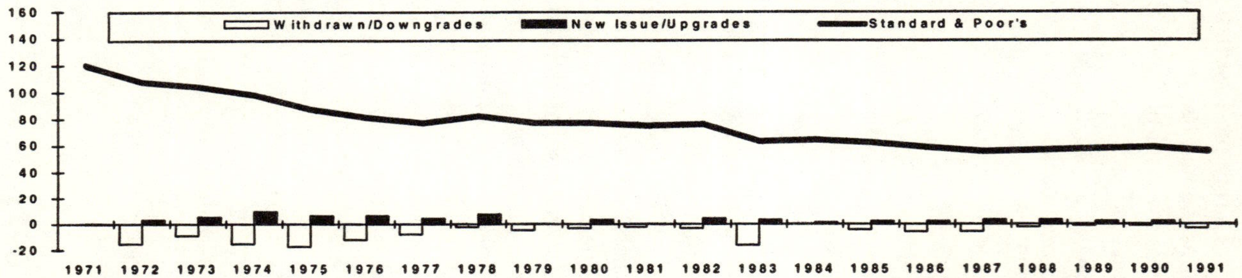

2. Standard & Poor's Corporation,"Muni Downgrades Fell Sharply in Second Quarter," *Standard & Poor's Creditweek*, July 20, 1992, p. 46.
3. Moody's Investors Service, "Municipal Bond Rating Revisions—1991," *Moody's Municipal Credit Report*, January 1992, p. 1.
4. Moody's Investors Service, "$5.6 Billion Affected by Second Quarter Municipal Bond Rating Revisions," *Moody's Public Finance Dept. Rating News*, July 10, 1992, p. 1.
5. Daniel Heimowitz and Edward Kerman, "Aaa Bonds," Moody's Investors Service-*Municipal Issues*, November/December 1989, pp. 6–8.
6. Moody's Investors Service, Public Finance Dept., *Municipal Focus on Counties*, July 1991, p. 5.
7. Moody's Investors Service, *Moody's Municipal Credit Report—State of California*, October 29, 1991, p. 3.

CHAPTER 4

TRIPLE-A RATING PROCESS

Triple-A rated issuers are members of an elite club. If you ask Moody's or S&P, they will simply say Triple-A issues are extremely strong and of the best quality. Moody's emphasizes that an Aaa is a measure of *absolute* quality.[1] If there are stronger or weaker financial attributes among issuers, the agencies usually rate the issues differently. In theory then, no interest rate differential should exist among Triple-A issues unless there is another explanation.

The normal place to look for the root of the interest rate differential is the process of earning this prestigious rating. At first glance, getting an insured rating might look easier since natural Triple-A's account for only 1 percent of the Triple-A issues while insured issues make up 70 percent.[2] This may be a result of the relative scarcity of natural Triple-A issuers and their fairly infrequent issuance. Conversely, in 1991 bond guarantors insured over 2,500 new issues. This pace has expanded the Triple-A population. Nonetheless, the statistics raise an important question: Do qualitative differences exist in the rating process? To pursue it, we will review the rating methods the major agencies use for both insured and natural bonds.

RATING THE NATURALS

What makes an issuer Triple-A in its own right? Moody's and S&P are not specific about the factors that give a particular bond their highest rating. However, let's look for guideposts among the key analytical factors and anecdotal evidence. When they review the different sectors of credit, rating agencies consider four broad areas—debt, the economy, the issuer's financial performance, and governmental administrative factors.

Since general obligation issues make up 87 percent of Moody's natural Triple-A's and 89 percent of S&P's, we will examine the rating process by looking at G.O.'s in particular.

Economic Factors

Since the taxes and fees that secure bonds are generated by the taxes of working people, the diversity and strength of the employment base are important benchmarks. Wealth and income indicators are measured against those of other similar cities, states, and counties. Full-value growth trends should show a consistent pattern for all taxable property and relate to factors such as population. Another essential component is an evaluation of the largest employers and taxpayers. In short, the natural Triple-A should reflect a strong, diversified economy with few, if any, weak sectors and no excessive reliance on any industry.

Debt Factors

Each issue must be reviewed with all the debt its tax base supports. This includes overlapping debt, such as the obligations of a school district and a municipal utility system, within the same tax base. Debt is measured in indicators, such as debt per capita, debt to full value and pro forma debt service to total expenditures. Also important is the percent of debt amortized in a 10-year period. In addition to the current total debt burden, the rating agencies also measure debt history and trends against the issuer's ability to pay. Any community targeting a Triple-A needs an effective planning program for capital improvements. The agencies also examine the structure of the community's debt, its reliance on variable-rate demand bonds, and the rate of debt retirement. Debt should fall within the limits imposed on the issuer.

Financial Factors

Besides reviewing statements of the community's operating results and year-end financial position, the rating agency analyst must be able to see these numbers in their broader context. Trends are important. Generally speaking, the issuer needs to generate a surplus in all but the direst of circumstances. There should be a solid general fund balance as a percent of revenues since these are financial reserves available for unforeseen contingencies. Budgets, plans, projections, and spending controls are necessary to maintain fiscal balance. Pension liabilities must be conservatively assessed and funded.

Administrative Factors

Since these factors are not easily quantifiable, they may be the most difficult to assess and compare. Critical areas are organization, division of responsibility, degree of professionalism, and authority consonant with responsibility. Effective tax collection, sound budgets, and prudent investments should already be part of the picture.

Moody's and Standard & Poor's have discussed these criteria at greater length in their own publications, *Moody's on Municipals* and *S&P's Municipal Finance Criteria*. While they describe what they analyze when looking at a Triple-A, they do not publish a formula for determining the rating. But written evaluations of downgraded issues suggest some elements involved in the review. Most common among downgrades are the accumulation of a substantial deficit and increased debt commitments. Here are representative observations from rating-agency publications when an issue was downgraded:

- Weakened financial operations the last three years and little expectation for change.
- Decline in key financial indicators and softness in the state's economy
- Chronic deficit operations and no budget reserves.
- Increased financial pressure both long and short term.
- The magnitude of the infrastructure needs and corresponding debt issuance.
- Spending demands of a rapidly growing population.
- Reduced revenue flexibility (voter tax revolts).
- Regional economic softening.
- Dependence on state aid.
- Declining fund balance.

Conversely, the reasons presented for upgrades to Triple-A focus on capacity to pay debt as measured by wealth, financial performance and debt load. Even issuers that may not meet some criteria, such as diversity of employment base, may earn a Triple-A if they are wealthy, well managed and have few liabilities. Low debt seems to be a key characteristic that is hard to achieve, which no doubt accounts for the scarcity of natural Triple-A issues.

In short, the major elements an issuer must possess to gain the Triple-A rating on its own merits are:

- High wealth indicators, low debt, comfortable margins of flexibility, and projections of superior financial performance. In lay terms, the agencies concentrate their attention on stability and capacity to pay and on margins of flexibility and protection.
- While standards for natural Triple-A's are clearly rigid and high, these issuers are not subjected to a formal stress test.

RATING THE BOND INSURER

What are the criteria for a Triple-A bond insurer? Moody's states that an insured Aaa "must have sufficient resources to pay all claims that might arise from a highly stressful scenario. They must also operate in a prudent manner so they avoid risk and continue to strengthen their claims-paying capacity. In other words, an Aaa municipal bond insurer must demonstrate both *large margins of protection and exceptional stability*."[3] (Emphasis added.)

S&P says "insurers rated 'AAA' offer superior financial security on both an absolute and relative basis. They possess the highest safety and have an overwhelming capacity to meet policyholder obligations."[4]

Both agencies scrutinize a bond insurer quantitatively and qualitatively. They review the balance sheet, earnings potential, and capital adequacy, as well as management, underwriting philosophy, and the quality of the insurer's portfolio and surveillance programs. They monitor premium rate levels to alert the agency analyst to any change in the risk/reward ratio. And, they carefully weigh the quality of reinsurance, and any so-called soft capital to evaluate the guarantor's long-term health.

However, the acid test begins with a strenuous measurement of capital adequacy. The agencies subject the business a company has insured to a depression scenario in which a percentage of the average annual debt service due in the "depression" goes into default. These defaults are translated into a "capital charge," which the rating agency assigns to each discrete bond sector to reflect the sector's relative risks. This capital charge represents the free capital an insurer should possess to support each insured issue and to meet obligations on a timely basis.

Both agencies base their capital charge methods on George Hempel's *The Post War Quality of State and Local Debt*. A key Hempel finding was a cumulative municipal bond default rate of 16 percent during the Great Depression that began in 1929. This rate, which is determined by dividing the principal and interest payments missed or overdue in the four- to five-year depression, by the period's aggregate average annual debt service, reflects estimates of actual market experience from 1929 to 1934. In other words, in a four- to five-year depression, a diversified portfolio could develop defaulted or overdue principal and interest that equaled the average annual principal and interest due during that depression.

It is important to emphasize that the 16 percent default rate is the average in a severe depression for all existing insured municipal bonds. Individual bond types of different underlying quality carry varying risks, have different default rates and therefore separate capital charges. For instance, in the S&P model, a state general obligation has an expected cumulative default rate of only 3 percent, the safest of any municipal bond. At the other extreme, a public power agency with substantial nuclear or special-project exposure has a rate of 40 percent, one of the highest risk categories for S&P. Currently, S&P's capital adequacy guidelines include 13 principal and 38 subcategories of municipal bonds. In S&P's depression test, the default rates apply to the weighted average annual debt service. The depression begins three or four years after the test begins.

Suppose, for example, that a bond guarantor was doing business in 1925 and guaranteed bonds until Black Thursday of October 1929. Then, through 1933, the guarantor developed a growing number of defaults, and began to recover. S&P's capital charge, which represents the percent of cumulative default rate, would increase as the depression wore on, in the way that it did from 1929 to 1933. Table 4–1 demonstrates the distribution of a state general obligation default.

Standard & Poor's developed its system of capital charges from Hempel's 16 percent Great Depression default rate. Using its own assessments, S&P added major refinements to reflect certain fundamental changes in the municipal market, primarily the shift away from the Great Depression-era's heavy reliance on general obligation debt to today's em-

TABLE 4–1
Standard & Poor's Depression Default Pattern for State General Obligation Municipal Bonds (Assumes a 3% Default Rate)

Year of Depression	*Percent of the Cumulative 3% Default Occurring in Each Year*	*Percent of Annual Default*	*Percent of Cumulative Default*
1st	7	.2	.2
2nd	11	.3	.5
3rd	30	.9	1.4
4th	52	1.6	3.0

phasis on generally higher-risk revenue bonds. S&P's model described in S&P's *CreditWeek* (1986), was designed to reflect the relative risk of the various issues insured, the likely duration of default in any sector, and the size of later losses.[5] All of these factors are expected to differ by issue type.

S&P's *CreditWeek* said that "the major refinement of the Hempel study was the identification of over 20 municipal sectors and the development of different capital 'charges' for each sector based upon the above." Because S&P capital charges presume that any insured bond will be investment grade, it does not further differentiate underlying credit quality. Generally, S&P assigns tailored capital charges to issues that are not investment grade; these can be 100 percent of the debt service due.

Moody's, which also used Hempel's conclusions, presented its model in 1988. While Moody's default or capital charge matrix has only nine principal bond categories, it does break out bonds in each sector by underlying credit strength. The range in capital charges runs from two percent for a Moody's Aaa-rated general obligation bond, to 60 percent for a corporate-backed municipal bond with less than a Baa rating.

Moody's further projects that a diverse portfolio of insured municipal bonds, guaranteed by one of the four major companies and rated at issuance, will develop cumulative default rates of 14 to 18 percent over a five-year depression scenario. The rate is derived by applying individual capital charges to each insurer's municipal bond portfolio.

Under Moody's stress test, the default rates by bond type and quality are expected to develop over five years instead of S&P's four. Interestingly, as Table 4–2 shows in the case of Moody's general obligation bonds, the percent of cumulative default increases more dramatically in

TABLE 4–2
Moody's Depression Default Pattern for General Obligation Bonds
(Assumes a 10% Default Rate)

Year of Depression	*Percent of the Cumulative 10% Default Occurring in Each Year*	*Percent of Annual Default*	*Percent of Cumulative Default*
1st	.1	0.10	0.01
2nd	.3	0.03	0.04
3rd	5.2	0.52	0.56
4th	42.0	4.20	4.76
5th	52.4	5.24	10.00

the depression's fourth year. See Table 4–2 for the distribution of default for a Moody's general obligation bond.

Moody's rating model for Triple-A municipal bond insurers embodies very conservative assumptions. In addition to subjecting the insurer to depression-type losses, it also allows for a substantial event risk by assuming that just before the depression the insurer suffers a permanent default on the average of the top 10 largest bond issues. Furthermore, it assumes that the insurer's investment portfolio loses value and some liquidity to rising interest rates, thus stressing both sides of the insurer's balance sheet.

Each agency's model helps determine how much capital is required to guarantee an insurer's payments on municipal bonds. At the same time, the model requires that the insurer remain solvent during the maximum stress of a Great Depression scenario. Both rating agency tests also insist that the insurer conclude the depression with enough capital to remain in the business of making bond guarantee commitments. The financial wherewithal to withstand such pressures should guarantee a "large margin of safety," Moody's stipulates in its Triple-A insurer criteria. These are very conservative tests in large part because the balance-sheet adequacy of U.S. cities and states on the eve of the Great Depression was not as good as it is today. State and local governments had labored under deficits since 1925, and in 1929 they began to buckle under the overwhelming burden of municipal debt, welfare, and public works. Figures 4–1 and 4–2 graph the surplus or deficit as a percent of revenues of all state and local governments and show state and local government debt to revenue leverage ratios.

FIGURE 4–1
State and Local Government Surplus or Deficit Percent of Revenue

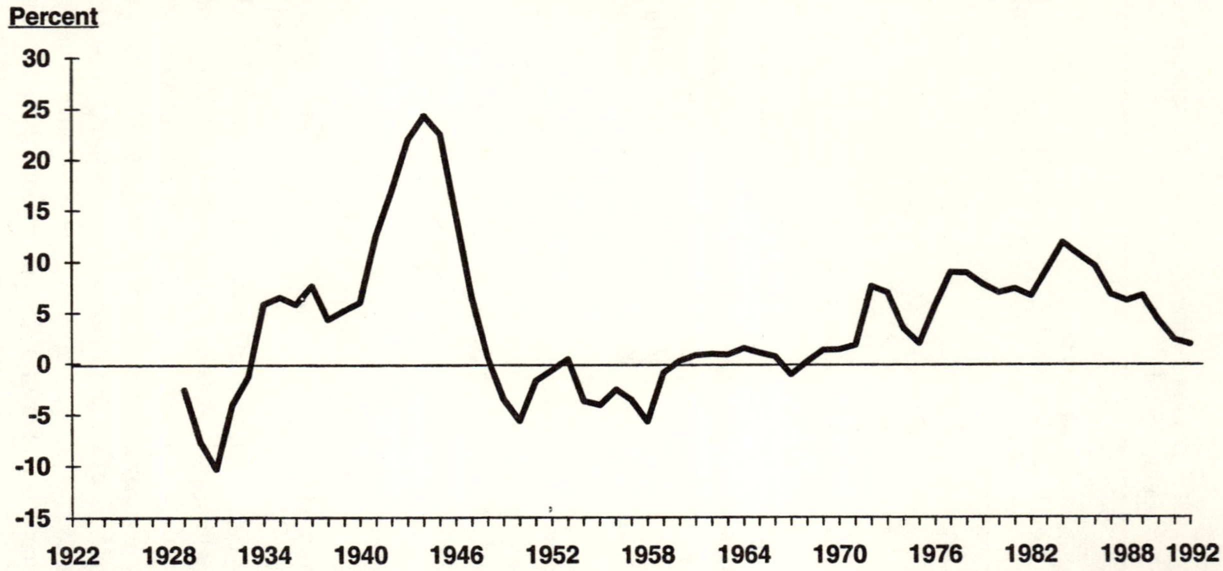

Source: Census Bureau and Fed Flow of Funds Accounts.

FIGURE 4–2
State and Local Government Debt to Revenue Leverage Ratios

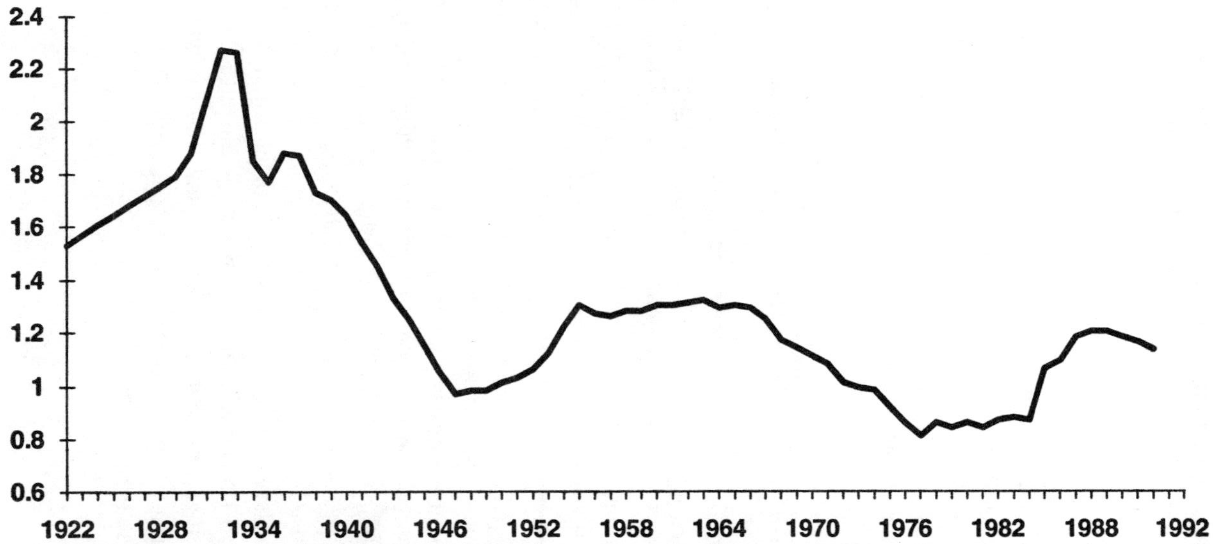

Source: Census Bureau and Fed Flow of Funds Accounts.

Municipal bond insurers absolutely must keep their Triple-A rating. Unlike a municipality or state, they do not have the luxury of losing the rating because the Triple-A is an essential requirement for remaining in business. And, in today's market, an insurer must have Triple-A ratings from both principal agencies to compete effectively. In contrast, a state or city with a natural Triple-A rating can elect to sacrifice that rating. If, for example, a city administration feels political pressure to incur deficits or hold the line on taxes, it can do so even though these steps might cost the city its Triple-A rating. The principal result: the city would pay slightly higher interest rates on its bond issues.

ANALYSIS AND CONCLUSION

During the last 20 years, the average life of a natural Triple-A has been eight to ten years. Only 16 Moody's and 18 S&P natural Triple-A's have kept their rating throughout the full 20-year period. Yet, on average, Moody's has rated over 120 Triple-A issuers each year and S&P rated over 60. In contrast, no monoline municipal-bond insurer has ever lost its Triple-A rating. Both natural and insured Triple-A's undergo very stringent rating processes. While natural Triple-A's do face difficult tests, natural and insured evaluations differ fundamentally. Insurers must survive a Great Depression scenario in which a mean of 16 percent of average annual debt service goes into default, while meeting all obligations on a timely basis. Although the naturals' evaluation may be intuitively as difficult, the rating agencies seem much more conservative with insurers. This stems from the industry's relative newness, the agencies' desire to lend a conservative bias to their assessment of guarantor strength and the fact that a downgrade of the insurer would affect many insured debt-holders. It is important to keep in mind the overwhelming number of outstanding bond issues that are rated Triple-A because of insurance rather than their natural quality.

NOTES

1. Daniel Heimowitz and Edward Kerman, "Aaa Bonds," *Municipal Issues*, Moody's Investors Service, Nov./Dec. 1989, pp. 6–8.
2. Ibid.

3. Moody's Investors Service, *Moody's on Municipals*, Moody's Investors Service, Inc., New York, 1991.
4. Standard & Poor's Insurance Rating Services, *S&P's Insurer Ratings List Claims-Paying Ability*, February 1992, p. 3.
5. Standard & Poor's Corporation, "Rating Methodology," *Standard & Poor's Credit Review—Bond Insurance*, December 15, 1986, pp. 4–6.

CHAPTER 5

NATURAL AND INSURED TRIPLE-A BONDS: THEIR FINANCIAL ATTRIBUTES

To make a proper assessment, we need to review the financial attributes of natural Triple-A issues, general municipal bonds, and insured issues. Let's look at the differences more closely to determine how significant they are and if they can explain trading values.

We have used Moody's 1992 Medians along with Census Bureau and Federal Reserve Flow of Funds Accounts data for the state and local government bond market statistics. For insured issues, we use data from Municipal Bond Investors Assurance Corporation, the largest municipal bond insurer, with an insured portfolio representative of the insured market. We gathered natural Triple-A data from the current list of issuers holding the highest rating from one or both of the major agencies.

NATURAL TRIPLE-A FINANCIAL ATTRIBUTES

Of the 141 natural Triple-A issuers of record on December 31, 1991, we obtained reasonably complete and current information on 98, or 70 percent, of the total. Of the issues reviewed, we obtained data on all 11 ot the higher education and 87 of the general obligation issuers. This information yielded nationwide aggregates for the personal income of the citizens, government revenues, and net debt outstanding.

Since the sample of 87 general obligation issuers accounts for 70 percent of the par value of outstanding natural Triple-A debt, and 4.7 percent of all public purpose, tax-exempt debt, it should accurately represent the full natural Triple-A market. Statistics generated by this sample should also compare favorably with the universe of state and local government bond issues. See Table 5–1.

TABLE 5–1
1991 Condensed Market Statistics of Natural Triple-A Bonds
(General Obligation and Tax-Backed Sector)

Critria	*Natural Triple-A Issues*	*Estimated Percent of National Statistics**
Personal income	$1,169.0 billion	23.7 percent
Governmental revenues	37.4 billion	4.8 percent
Overall net debt	41.0 billion	4.7 percent

*Percentage may be high due to redundancies caused by overlapping jurisdictions.

Source: Issuer Official Statement Data; Federal Reserve *Flow of Funds Accounts; Statistical Abstract of the United States.*

Earlier, we observed that natural Triple-A's are affluent. Low debt or leverage ratios are also key traits. Our research confirmed this; natural Triple-A's are located in areas of high personal income and relatively low debt. Net tax-supported debt per capita is almost equal to the national average. However, when gross state and local government debt per capita is calculated, the natural Triple-A's are nearly 86 percent less leveraged.

Let us review further the 87 general obligation issues. From the data, we have abstracted in Table 5–2 the key credit criteria of the natural Triple-A's and compared them to the arithmetic mean of the Moody's 1992 Medians (indicators by state for the 1991 year), which is one of the more widely recognized industry sources on municipal credit and believed to be indicative of state and local government performance statistics. In Table 5–3 we compared additional aggregate data.

Two more statistics drive home natural Triple-A strength—net debt to full value and full value per capita. Natural Triple-A's have over 38 percent less debt to full value (taxable properties) while their full value per capita is nearly 65 percent greater than national averages. Recall, however, that full value is an estimate that may not be current, fully reflect economic reality, or compare from region to region. Finally, though full value represents wealth, it does not necessarily indicate income production, the primary source of debt payments.

Still, when income and cash flow measures are analyzed, natural Triple-A's excel again. While net debt to personal income is only 18.5 percent below the mean of the Moody's Median, aggregate debt is more than 86 percent below the national average. Gross state and local government debt, only 2.4 percent of personal income for natural Triple-A's, is

TABLE 5–2
1991 Natural Triple-A/Moody's Medians Comparisons*

Criteria	*Natural Triple-A Results*	*Arithmetic Mean of Moody's Median*	*Natural Triple-A Variance*
Net tax-supported debt/capita	$542	$536	+1.1%
Net tax-supported debt/estimated full value	0.8%	1.3%	−38.4%
Net tax-supported debt/personal income	2.2%	2.7%	−18.5%
Estimated full value/capita	$65,356	$39,696	+64.6%

*As represented by the arithmetic mean of the Moody's Median.

Source: Issuer Official Statement Data; Moody's Public Finance Department, 1992.

far below the 17.6 percent for the country as a whole. Personal income per capita is strong, with natural Triple-A's 22 percent higher than the national average.

One more consistent fact emerges. Natural Triple-A's, due to their affluence, even under-leverage their tax revenue base more than the nation at large. Gross debt to government revenue is nearly 3 percent below that average, which aligns completely with the income and cash flow indicators of tax-paying citizens, and when seen as part of government income statement performance. Naturals not only balance their budgets well, but they also earn a respectable surplus, estimated at 9.4 percent of revenues in 1991. In contrast, all state and local government ran at a 3.4 percent deficit when social insurance funds were deleted.

When we compare the colleges and universities that make up the remaining 6 percent of the natural Triple-A bond group with the higher education institutions, we will review four key numbers—revenues, expenses, surplus or deficit, and endowment. They will profile this sector's basic financial health and ability to service debt. Although current and complete aggregate revenue data are unavailable, we have enough information from the U.S. Department of Education to make reasonable esti-

TABLE 5–3
Natural Triple-A Credit and Income Statistics

1991 Supplemental Credit Comparisons

Criteria	*Natural Triple-A Results*	*Nationwide Averages*	*Natural Triple-A Variance*
Gross state and local debt/capita	$573	$3,493	−83.6%
Estimated personal income/capita	$24,174	$19,875	+21.6%
Gross state and local government debt/personal income	2.4%	17.6%	−86.4%
Gross state and local debt to revenues	1.10:1	1.13:1	−2.7%

*1991 Condensed Income Statement Statistics**

	Natural Triple-A's	*All State and Local Governments*	*Naturals as % of Total*
Revenues	$37.4 billion	$771.7 billion	4.8%
Expenses	$33.9 billion	$798.3 billion	4.2%
Surplus (deficit)	$ 3.5 billion	$(26.6 billion)	N/A
Surplus (deficit)% of revenues	9.4%	(3.4%)	N/A

*Net of social insurance funds.

Source: Issuer Official Statement Data; Federal Reserve *Flow of Funds Accounts*; *Statistical Abstract of the U.S.–1991*; Moody's Public Finance Department *1992 Medians.*

mates. We have reliable endowment information from *The Chronicle of Higher Education*, covering the 395 largest colleges and universities, which represent an estimated 95 percent of all endowment funds. Topping the list is Harvard, with $4.7 billion in 1991; Indiana University of Pennsylvania (located in Indiana, PA) completes the list with just $2.053 million.

TABLE 5–4
1991 College and University Comparison

Criteria	*Natural Triple-A's*	*Colleges/Universities in Aggregate (est.)*
Revenues	$4.155 billion	$153.6 billion
Expenses	$3.842 billion	$164.0 billion
Surplus (Deficit)	$ 313 million	$(10.4 billion)
	7.5%	(6.8%)
Endowment	$14.837 billion	$ 64.5 billion

Source: Official Statements of Natural Triple-A colleges and universities; U.S. Department of Education–National Center for Educational Statistics; *The Chronicle of Higher Education.*

Virtually all of the natural Triple-A institutions manage their financial resources well and are operating on a profitable basis, while colleges and universities in total generate a significant deficit. Moreover, natural Triple-A's have about 23 percent of total U.S. endowment but only about 3 percent of revenues. See Table 5–4.

To this point, all natural Triple-A data have borne out the criteria we set forth in Chapter 4 for natural Triple-A's. Bond issuers that have achieved Triple-A ratings on their own merits have done it with low leverage, high wealth, and cash flow. As a group, they stand out from the market, particularly the issuers in higher education.

INSURED TRIPLE-A ATTRIBUTES

How do natural Triple-A's compare to a typical insured Triple-A portfolio? Our insured bond market data are drawn from MBIA's portfolio statistics at year-end 1991. MBIA had insured $184.6 billion, 36.9 percent of the industry's $500.2 billion in financial guarantees.[1] Table 5–5 compares MBIA's bond type distribution with that of the bond insurance industry at large.

We will review only MBIA's tax-backed and general obligation and higher education segments to allow us to compare them directly with natural Triple-A's. More comprehensive credit analysis on the entire MBIA portfolio versus natural Triple-A's will be discussed in Chapter 6.

At the end of 1991, MBIA had insured 9,992 tax-backed and general obligation issues and 904 higher education institution bonds. For this

TABLE 5–5
Insured Bond Type Distribution, 1991*

Bond Type	*MBIA % Par Value*	*All Insurers % of Par Value Insured*
General obligation and other tax-backed	33%	36%
Utilities (including corp.)	18	19
Hospitals	22	13
Colleges/universities	6	4
Transportation	6	6
Special revenue	8	4
Asset-backed	4	15
All other	3	3
	100%	100%

*MBIA's bond type distribution by par volume insured compared to the total insured market.

Source: AFGI 1991 Annual Report; MBIA data.

TABLE 5–6
1991 Condensed Market Statistics on Natural and Insured Triple-A Bonds

Criteria	*Insured Bonds**	*Naturals*
Personal income	\$1,806 billion	\$1,169 billion
Governmental revenues	64.6 billion	37.4 billion
Overall net debt	74.5 billion†	41.0 billion

*Compiled and calculated from the MBIA tax-backed and G.O. sample data.
†Overall net debt also includes other outstanding issuer debt not insured by MBIA.

study, we used 3,561 tax-backed and general obligation issues and 71 higher education issues.[2]

First, we compare the condensed market statistics of the insured tax-backed and general obligation bonds with the natural Triple-A's in Table 5–6 and more detailed credit comparisons in Table 5–7.

In personal income, revenues, and debt, insured issues mirror the natural Triple-A's. In relative terms, leverage is low and personal income high.

How do natural and insured bonds compare with each other and with Moody's Medians, particularly on a per capita basis? At first glance at the data in Table 5–7, insured bonds appear significantly more leveraged

TABLE 5–7
1991 Triple-A/Moody's Medians Comparisons

Criteria	*Insured Triple-A Results*	*Natural Triple-A Results*	*Arithmetic Mean of Moody's Median*	*Variance/ Insured/ Naturals*	*Variance/ Insured/ Moody's*	*Variance/ Naturals/ Moody's*
Net tax-supported debt/capita	$1,227	$542	$536	+126%	+128%	+1%
Net tax-supported debt/full value	3.1%	0.8%	1.3%	+288%	+138%	−38%
Net tax-supported debt/personal income	4.1%	2.2%	2.7%	+86%	+52%	−18%
Estimated full value/capita	$40,186	$65,356	$39,696	−39%	+1%	+65%

Source: MBIA Data; Issuer Official Statements: Federal Reserve *Flow of Funds Accounts*; *Statistical Abstract of the U.S.—1991*, Moody's Public Finance Department *1992 Medians*.

than either the naturals or the general market. The hefty $1,227 per capita net debt figure is more than double the other two categories and, as such, produces much higher ratios of debt to full value and personal income. Moreover, the insured portfolio full value is essentially the same per capita as the national statistic and below the wealthier $65,356 per capita of the naturals.

However, when we compare other figures in Table 5–8, a much clearer financial picture emerges. For example, in gross debt per capita numbers, the naturals still excel, but the insureds are 56 percent below estimated national averages. The insured bonds' distinguishing strength is personal income per capita. It stands a very significant 23 percent above the naturals and 50 percent over the countrywide average, indicating the insured sector's strong underlying earning power. Gross debt as a percent of personal income is still higher than the naturals, but also well under national numbers, and debt to governmental revenue leverage ratios are virtually the same for all three categories.

Table 5–8 contains some of the most important credit variables in terms of measuring an issuer's ability to repay debt, and, to the naked eye, the naturals do not look overwhelmingly better than the insured bond group. To determine if the differences are meaningful, let's perform a statistical significance test (see calculation details in the Appendix). Using a difference in means test, we found there was no significant difference between the naturals and the insured bond group in the categories of personal income per capita, the gross debt to personal income ratio, and the debt to governmental revenue leverage ratios. There was a statistically significant difference (albeit slight) on debt per capita, but this finding is not unexpected.

In budget performance, insureds again almost rival the naturals, posting a healthy surplus of 7.3 percent of revenues versus 9.4 percent for naturals and a 3.4 percent nationwide deficit. Further analysis showed that insured bonds compare very favorably with naturals in financial and risk management. On a current tax-collections basis, insured bond issuers collect 95.1 percent versus 96.7 percent for the naturals. Insured issues exceed the naturals in total collections with a 99.0 percent performance versus 97.8 percent for naturals, all very good records. Naturals have only 7.72 percent of their assessments concentrated in the top five taxpayers, while insured issues have 10.74 percent. Although the insured group is higher, both ratios are exemplary and show desirable diffusion with a diversity of tax base. Over the next 15 years, naturals are sched-

TABLE 5–8
Triple-A Credit and Income Statistics

1991 Supplemental Credit Comparisons

Criteria	*Insured Bonds*	*Natural Triple-A's*	*Nationwide Averages*	*Variance/ Insured/ Naturals*	*Variance/ Insured/ Nationwide*
Gross state and local debt/capita	$ 1,543	$ 573	$ 3,493	+169%	−56%
Estimated personal Income/capita	$29,763	$24,174	$19,875	+23%	+50%
Gross state and local government debt/estimated personal income	5.1%	2.4%	17.6%	+113%	−71%
Gross state and local debt to revenues	1.16:1*	1.10:1	1.13:1	+5%	+3%

1991 Condensed Income Statement Statistics†

	*Insured Bonds**	*Natural Triple-A's*	*All State and Local Governments*
Revenues	$64.4 billion	$37.4 billion	$771.7 billion
Expenses	$59.7 billion	$33.9 billion	$798.3 billion
Surplus (deficit)	$4.7 billion	$3.5 billion	($26.6 billion)
Surplus (deficit) % of revenues	7.3%	9.4%	(3.4%)

*Compiled and calculated from the MBIA tax-backed and general obligation sample data.

†Net of social insurance funds.

Source: MBIA data; Issuer Official Statements: Federal Reserve *Flow of Funds Accounts*; *Statistical Abstract of the U.S.—1991*, Moody's Public Finance Department *1992 Medians.*

uled to retire 85.6 percent of their debt. Among MBIA's tax-backed and general obligation issues, the states will retire at a slightly higher rate of 87.3 percent, with 81.3 percent retired among municipalities and 79.2 percent by counties. This performance is roughly comparable for both sectors.

Our data review tells us that insured state and local government debt issues generally represent growing regions and communities that are experiencing strains that accompany growth, particularly higher debt. While the benefits of their investments are yet to come, their incomes are outstanding, exceeding all other sectors. In short, the insured sector resembles the young family with a good income but higher debt because it is buying capital goods. For these issuers, the advantage of bond insurance is the cost savings made possible by the insurer's Triple-A ratings. Despite higher debt levels, the insured sector manages its budgets as well as the naturals by posting healthy surpluses, all the more remarkable since the insured issuers are growing steadily. In spot-checking the sample groups, only 16.5 percent of the issues showed current-year deficits.

Turning to higher education, how do the insured bonds compare with natural Triple-A's? Answer: reasonably well. Table 5–9 presents key financial data on the natural Triple-A's and the 71-member sample of MBIA's book of 285 issuers of higher education and related bonds.

Insured surplus margins are not as healthy as the naturals, but they far surpass the national average, an aggregate deficit of $10.4 billion. Debt-to-revenue ratio is actually better for the insured issues. However, the naturals excel in their endowments and debt-to-endowment ratios because of the fund's size.

Overall, each group of issuers has strong credit fundamentals. It is clear that the strength of the naturals is their endowments, which enable them to operate at a surplus.

CONCLUSIONS

Natural Triple-A's in the tax-backed and general obligation and higher education sectors have credit fundamentals similar to insured bonds. Pure indeed members of an elite financial club. However, which category of Triple-A bonds is undeniably better remains an open question. More important, bond investors must remember that the favorable ratios of the natural issues are essentially their only protection. The slightly less favor-

TABLE 5–9

Insured versus Natural Triple-A/1991 Higher Education Sector Comparisons

Criteria	*Total*	*Natural Triple-A's Avg./School*	*Total*	*Insured Bonds Avg./School*
Revenues	$4.155 billion	$ 378 million	$14.044 billion	$198 million
Expenses	$3.842 billion	$ 349 million	$13.755 billion	$194 million
Surplus (deficit)	$ 313 million	$ 28 million	$ 289 million	$ 4 million
Surplus (deficit) % of revenues	7.5%		2.1%	
Endowment or fund balance	$14.837 billion	$1.349 billion	$6.500 billion	$ 92 million
Debt outstanding	$ 1.979 billion	$ 180 million	$4.446 billion*	$ 63 million
Debt to revenue	0.48:1		0.32:1	
Debt to endowment or fund balance	0.13:1		0.68:1	

*Includes debt not insured by MBIA.

Source: Official Statements of Natural Triple-A Colleges and Universities, MBIA company data.

able underlying attributes of insured bonds are offset by the bond insurer's added strength in the form of its asset portfolio.

The asset portfolios of these guarantors must be used first to pay any defaults that occur on any insured bond. This extra layer of protection, which has already survived close scrutiny by the rating agencies, further enhances the value of an already strong portfolio of underlying obligations. We need to go further to discover why the naturals have historically enjoyed a significantly lower interest rate than their insured counterparts. In the next chapter, we analyze the added strength a bond insurer brings to an issue in times of stress and critically examine how well the bond insurer can fulfill its promise.

NOTES

1. AFGI, 1991, MBIA Inc., Annual Report, 1991.
2. It is believed these samples are fully indicative of the entire MBIA book of insured issues in these two business segments. A more detailed description of these data and the remaining sample of MBIA's portfolio used in Chapter 6 will be presented in that section.

CHAPTER 6

PROJECTED FINANCIAL PERFORMANCE UNDER STRESS

Performance under severe economic stress is the test of every bond. In other words, can it meet principal and interest payment on time in a recession or depression? Because of the research done for *Risk Based Capital Charges for Municipal Bonds*, we can apply an econometric test based on the Great Depression (1929–1938) to any type of municipal bond.[1] Thus far, that decade has been the worst economic calamity for bonds in the last 150 years. Sixty-six percent of all bond defaults since 1869 occurred during that period. Any bond that can survive that magnitude of stress should perform well in normal economic times. Any defaulting bond should be among the worst.

Bonds default for two reasons: (1) the issuer runs out of funds and (2) it cannot obtain liquidity. In a depression or recession, a bond issuer's revenues tend to go down and expenses follow—but more slowly. Operating deficits result, and issuers who lack a cash cushion must find liquidity, available to only the most creditworthy borrowers, and then only in limited amounts. Issuers who cannot obtain liquidity risk defaulting on their bond obligations.

As we apply Great Depression economics to natural Triple-A's and MBIA-insured bonds, the results will demonstrate whether one group is superior. If the two groups compare in strength, we will know that risk concerns are not causing the yield differential between them.

NATURAL TRIPLE-A STRESS PERFORMANCE

Starting with tax-backed and general obligation bonds, which comprised 94 percent of the naturals in 1991, we asked, "What would happen to the performance of these issuers if the Great Depression happened again in January 1992? Would these bonds remain healthy or default? If they defaulted, when would they default, and by how much?" Before starting the test, it would be helpful to go back and observe the revenue, deficit, and additional debt issuance patterns for general obligation issuers from the Great Depression, as shown in Table 6–1.

Before we stress the aggregate statistics of our natural Triple-A's, let's recall their key financial attributes. Total revenues for the sample's latest year were $37.4 billion, which includes taxes, fees, and related amounts. The incoming fund balance, roughly equal to the cash cushion available to absorb any deficits, is estimated at $6.5 billion. Current debt outstanding is $41 billion and estimated average annual debt service is $3.745 billion, with principal estimated at $1.6 billion.

While the naturals fare very well, they are not trouble free. In year six (see Table 6–2), deficits in years one through five and shrinking liquidity in years five and six combine to produce an overall negative fund balance estimated at $100 million. That portion of the estimated annual debt service of $3.745 billion could not be paid and defaults of this size would result. The $100 million equates to 2.6 percent of the average annual debt service (100 divided by $3745) and compares favorably to the cumulative 16 percent of the average annual debt service that defaulted in

TABLE 6–1
Depression-Era Revenue, Deficit, and Debt Patterns for All State and Local Governments

Year	*Percent Change in Revenues from Prior Year*	*Surplus(Deficit) Percent of Revenues*	*Percent Increase in Debt Outstanding from Prior Year*
1929	Base year	(2.6)	7.1
1930	+2.6	(7.7)	8.1
1931	−1.3	(10.3)	8.8
1932	−5.2	(4.1)	3.8
1933	−1.4	(1.4)	(1.8)
1934	+19.4	5.8	(2.5)
1935	+5.8	6.5	1.3
1936	−5.5	5.8	0.6
1937	+5.8	7.7	(0.6)
1938	+2.2	4.3	—

Source: *Risk Based Capital Charges for Municipal Bonds* (1990); U.S. Bureau of the Census (1975).

TABLE 6–2
Depression Stress Test of Natural Triple-A Tax-Backed and General Obligation Bonds ($ Billions)

Year	*Revenues*	*Surplus (Deficit)*	*Net Increase (Decrease) in Debt*	*Estimated Annual Debt Service**	*Resulting Cumulative Fund Balance at Year-End*
1	$37.4	$(0.97)	$2.9	$1.6	$6.8
2	38.4	(2.96)	3.6	1.6	5.9
3	37.9	(3.90)	4.2	1.6	4.6
4	35.9	(1.47)	2.0	1.6	3.5
5	35.4	(0.50)	(1.0)	1.6	0.4
6	42.3	2.45	(1.3)	1.6	(0.1)
7	44.7	2.91	0.7	1.6	2.0
8	42.3	2.45	0.3	1.6	3.1
9	44.7	3.44	(0.3)	1.6	4.7
10	45.7	1.97	—	1.6	5.0

*Principal portion only—interest portion is included in surplus (deficit).

the Great Depression.[2] Moreover, it is consistent with the 2 percent estimated Depression default rate (capital charge) for a Moody's Triple-A rated general obligation bond and a comparable 3 percent state (and 10 percent city/county) Standard & Poor's general obligation capital charge.

Of the 87 issues tested, 39 suffered default problems in the stress test, somewhat more than actually defaulted in the Depression. However, many of the 39 had only very minor amounts defaulting. The total defaulted dollar amount is much better than in 1929 because of stronger balance sheets, greater liquid assets, and less overall debt at the state and local government levels. Overall, the naturals would perform very well in another Great Depression, but they would not be perfect.

Let us now subject natural Triple-A college and university bonds to the same test. During periods of economic pressure, people tend to spend more on education as they seek training to develop new skills and become more marketable. However, since higher educational institutions are in oversupply, the stress test does not use actual education spending figures for the Great Depression. Instead, to lend a more conservative bias to the test, it employs the more conservative pattern for the rate of fall in personal income. Since education costs tend to be paid from personal income, this method gives education an equal opportunity with other components in the consumption category. See Table 6–3.

TABLE 6–3
Depression-Era Changes in Personal Income

Year	*Percent Change from Prior Year*
1929	Base year
1930	−10.4%
1931	−14.3
1932	−23.6
1933	−6.3
1934	+14.7
1935	+12.6
1936	+13.7
1937	+7.9
1938	−7.9

Source: U.S. Bureau of the Census (1975).

The stress model estimates that operating expenses also fall, but at a rate 15 percent slower than revenues, which mirrors actual Great Depression experience on a compound basis. Endowments or fund balances, invested in a mix of marketable securities, would cover deficits. During the Great Depression, school endowments actually *increased* at a compound rate of 2.09 percent from 1930 through 1938. We will conservatively presume endowment funds do not grow during the test. We will also presume the schools would not issue any new debt. To recap key financial attributes, the naturals have current annual revenues of $4.155 billion, expenses of $3.842 billion, and endowments valued at $14.837 billion. Debt outstanding is $1.979 billion and the estimated principal portion of annual debt service is $79.2 million.

Not surprisingly, as Table 6–4 shows, the naturals weather the depression scenario without touching their endowments' principal. That is less astonishing when you consider how large the endowments are, and when you look at their track records in different economic climates. At least one of the naturals, Harvard, has made it through the 12 U.S. recessions and depressions since the Civil War. In fact, it survived not only the Civil War but also the Revolutionary War and the country's three forms of central government since settlers came to North America.

In summary, the naturals could survive a Great Depression with relatively modest defaults in general obligation and tax-backed bonds, and no defaults among the higher education issues.

TABLE 6–4
Depression Stress Test of Natural Triple-A Colleges and Universities ($ Billions)

Year	*Revenues*	*Expenses*	*Surplus (Deficit)*	*Estimated Annual Debt Service**	*Cumulative Operating Surplus (Deficit) after Debt Service before Endowment Adjustments*
1	$4.155	$3.842	$0.313	$0.079	$0.234
2	3.723	3.503	0.220	0.079	0.375
3	3.191	3.076	0.115	0.079	0.411
4	2.438	2.461	(0.023)	0.079	0.309
5	2.284	2.328	(0.044)	0.079	0.186
6	2.620	2.619	0.001	0.079	0.108
7	2.950	2.900	0.050	0.079	0.079
8	3.354	3.236	0.118	0.079	0.118
9	3.619	3.453	0.166	0.079	0.205
10	3.333	3.221	0.112	0.079	0.238

*Principal portion only—interest is included in expenses.

INSURED BONDS STRESS PERFORMANCE

Should we expect insured bonds to perform like the naturals? Before we stress-test MBIA's portfolio of insured bonds to compare them with the natural Triple-A's, let us review precisely what a bond insurer does. MBIA, in this case, stands in the shoes of the bond issuers when it insures a bond. If the issuer cannot make timely principal and interest payments, MBIA takes over and makes those payments until the issuer can resume them—if ever. Therefore, the buyer of an MBIA-insured bond is protected not only by the resources of the entity which issued the bond, but also by the resources of MBIA. In addition, in the event of a default, holders of MBIA-insured bonds have first claim on all MBIA assets before any other creditor or stockholder of the company (we will discuss resources and assets later in this chapter). First, let us stress-test MBIA's insured portfolio on a comparable basis with the naturals.

At the end of 1991, MBIA had net insurance outstanding of $90 billion par value and $184.6 billion for both principal and interest obligations on a total of 24,250 separate bond issues insured since MBIA's inception. See Table 6–5.

TABLE 6–5
MBIA Portfolio Distribution as of 12/31/91 ($ Billions)

Bond Type	*Number of Issues*	*Number of Issuers*	*Net Par Outstanding*	*Net Principal and Interest Outstanding*
G.O. and tax-backed	9,992	3,599	$36.7	$ 66.1
Health care	2,743	593	17.5	38.6
Utilities—municipal and corporate	6,331	1,062	17.8	40.2
Higher education	904	285	4.1	8.3
Other special revenue	1,756	151	6.7	14.8
Housing/structured finance	2,524	569	7.2	16.6
Totals	24,250	6,259	$90.0	$184.6

As with the natural Triple-A's, the test will determine the likely times and amounts of Great Depression defaults that would occur among MBIA's insured issues by applying the stress of falling revenues, resulting deficits, and constrained liquidity to a representative sample of MBIA's 6,259 separate insured issuers. Sample results will be generalized to the portfolio at large.

Issue data were gathered from two MBIA databases: the Underwriting System and Surveillance Reviews. The Underwriting System is maintained for tax-backed and general obligation issues; Surveillance Reviews cover health care, utilities, and higher education bonds. Together, these databases comprise 100 percent of the available information, which includes current issuer financial statements in enough detail to perform cash flow stress tests and financial analysis.

The Underwriting System for tax-backed and general obligation issues contained data on 3,561 issues approved by MBIA for the 18 months preceding the start of this study in early 1992. It represents a 100 percent sample of the insurable issues MBIA reviewed during that time. MBIA has insured 9,992 tax-backed and general obligation issues since it was established in 1974. We believe the review sample is reasonably large and diverse enough to represent the financial characteristics of the entire portfolio of tax-backed and general obligation issues. While the sample does cover only a recent period in MBIA history, it is a complete and unedited sample. It's also worth noting that the issuer's financial statements occurred in a recession, which may lend the data a further conservative bias.

Data on the other bond types were gathered from summaries of MBIA's Surveillance Reviews. MBIA's Surveillance Department has reviewed and compiled relatively complete financial data on 465 issuers (out of a total of 1,940 issuers insured) in health care, higher education, and utilities. These reviews first analyzed any issuer MBIA had assigned a lower credit rating, along with any larger issuer in terms of MBIA exposure. In addition, newly insured health care issues were encoded into the database, which in total provided a mix of lower-rated credits, larger issues, and new business with potentially higher credit ratings. The linear average internal credit rating for the health care issuers was a 3.05, versus 2.98 for MBIA's overall book of health care bonds, as of year-end 1991. The 2.98 to 3.05 rating is the general equivalent of an A rating from Moody's and Standard & Poor's. The 3.05 for the sample is only slightly below the rating for all health-care issues and is not statistically significant.

The higher education issuers in the sample generate a linear average internal credit rating of 4.9 versus 3.18 for MBIA's total book of higher education business. The 4.9 rating roughly equals a Baa/BBB from the rating agencies, while the 3.18 is still equal to an A. Utility bond ratings for the sample were not available. However, we believe this sample, too, is large enough to represent MBIA's overall portfolio. Indeed, the higher education issues may actually give a more conservative picture of financial statistics due to the skewing to lower-rated credits. Two sectors lack sufficient data to do cash-flow-based econometric stress testing. These are the non-higher education portion of special revenue issues which amount to 8 percent of total debt service, and housing and structured finance issues, 9 percent of total debt service. For these, we will use rating agency models to provide a reasonable estimate of potential claims.

In total, all issuers in the sample comprise a total estimated tax-exempt debt of $102.9 billion par value as of year-end 1991. This is 10.6 percent of the $968.1 billion in tax-exempt debt outstanding at year-end 1991 for all state and local governments and non-profit enterprises.

Before dealing with each bond type, we should review MBIA's insured debt service schedule for the test period from 1992 through 2001. Table 6–6 displays it by bond type and in total.

TABLE 6–6
MBIA Insured Net Debt Service Exposure Schedule/Depression Test Period—1992/2001 ($ Millions)

Year	*Tax-Backed*	*Structured Finance*	*Corporate and Municipal Utilities*	*Health Care*	*Other Special Revenue*	*Special Revenue/ Higher Education*	*Total*
1992	$4,059	$1,173	$1,557	$1,484	$541	$348	$9,162
1993	3,966	1,120	1,680	1,596	607	363	9,332
1994	3,924	1,080	1,629	1,565	586	366	9,150
1995	3,887	1,094	1,651	1,623	590	378	9,223
1996	3,749	847	1,693	1,552	617	362	8,820
1997	3,607	847	1,747	1,538	621	376	8,736
1998	3,663	766	1,749	1,523	627	374	8,702
1999	3,451	744	1,751	1,539	609	364	8,458
2000	3,384	665	1,700	1,503	608	353	8,213
2001	3,285	612	1,723	1,474	612	346	8,052

Source: MBIA company reports.

Tax-Backed and General Obligation Insured Issues

MBIA's tax-backed and general obligation insured issues comprise the largest book of business, with 9,992 separate issues for 3,599 different issuers. Test data were gathered from 3,561 issues, which represent MBIA's overall portfolio of tax-backed and general obligation issues. A quick recap shows the sample's estimated vital statistics as $64.4 billion in current year revenues; $74.5 billion in overall net debt outstanding (includes other issuer debt not insured by MBIA); $14.7 billion in incoming fund balance; and $3.5 billion as the principal portion of annual debt service.

When we applied the depression stress test to tax-backed and general-obligation debt on an aggregated basis, we applied the same assumptions and methods that were applied to the natural Triple-A's. MBIA's issues ran into trouble meeting debt service in the sixth year, the same year as the natural Triple-A's. The sample develops a deficit fund balance of about $200 million, which would result in the default of an equal amount of debt service. See Table 6–7 for results. Of the issues, 29.5 percent or 1,051 experience default, most of it relatively minoı While

TABLE 6–7
Depression Stress Test of MBIA Tax-Backed and General Obligation Bonds
($ Billions)

Year	*Revenues*	*Surplus (Deficit)*	*Net Increase (Decrease) in Debt*	*Estimated Annual Debt Service**	*Resulting Cumulative Fund Balance Year-End*
1	$64.4	$(1.7)	$5.3	$3.5	$14.8
2	66.1	(5.1)	6.5	3.5	12.7
3	65.2	(6.7)	7.6	3.5	10.1
4	61.8	(2.5)	3.6	3.5	7.7
5	61.0	(0.9)	(1.8)	3.5	1.5
6	72.8	4.2	(2.4)	3.5	(0.2)
7	77.0	5.0	1.2	3.5	2.5
8	72.8	4.2	0.6	3.5	3.8
9	77.0	5.9	(0.6)	3.5	5.6
10	78.7	3.4	—	3.5	5.5

*Principal portion only—interest included in surplus (deficit).

not as strong as the natural Triple-A's, the insured bonds still perform relatively well on their own.

Natural Triple-A's started the depression test with a fund balance equal to an average 17.4 percent of first-year revenues and the insured sample began with a healthier 22.8 percent. However, with their higher debt, the insured bonds had a debt service burden (principal portion percentage) of 5.4 percent of revenues at the start of the test while the natural Triple-A's had 4.3 percent. The naturals' lower leverage overcame their initial smaller fund balance—this is demonstrated even further in test year five. Taking the principal portion of debt service burden as a percent of revenues, the ratio for the naturals moves up to only 4.5 percent versus 5.7 percent for the insured bonds. At the test's end, the naturals' cumulative fund balances were 10.9 percent of year 10 revenues versus seven percent for the insured bonds. The test makes clear that because of their higher debt burdens, insured issues deteriorate slightly more than naturals and do not recover as well.

With annual principal and interest debt service estimated at $6.3 billion, the defaulting amount of insured bonds equals 3.2 percent of annual debt service compared with 2.6 percent for the natural Triple-A's. Extrapolating this finding to MBIA's overall tax-backed and general obligation business, defaults in this sector would amount to $115.4 million in the sixth year, or 3.2 percent of $3.607 billion of tax-backed and general obligation debt service.

Higher Education

Among the higher education issuers, we sampled 71 of MBIA's 258. Briefly, this bond group's current year revenues are $14.044 billion; current year expenses, $13.755 billion; debt outstanding, $4.446 billion (includes debt not insured by MBIA); and endowment or fund balances, $6.5 billion.

Again, we made the same model assumptions as we did with the natural Triple-A's. And, like the naturals, the insured colleges and universities can survive a Great Depression without a default, although their endowment and fund balances would be severely drained. Here again, no fundamental difference exists between insured and natural Triple-A bonds. See Table 6–8.

TABLE 6–8
Depression Stress Test of MBIA Higher Education Bonds ($ Billions)

Year	*Revenues*	*Expenses*	*Surplus (Deficit)*	*Estimated Debt Service**	*Resulting Cumulative Endowment or Fund Balance at Year-End*
1	$14.044	$13.755	$ .289	$.178	$6.611
2	12.583	12.544	.039	.182	6.468
3	10.784	11.014	(.230)	.184	6.054
4	8.239	8.811	(.572)	.190	5.292
5	7.720	8.335	(.615)	.182	4.495
6	8.855	9.377	(.522)	.189	3.784
7	9.970	10.380	(.410)	.188	3.186
8	11.336	11.585	(.249)	.183	2.754
9	12.232	12.361	(.129)	.177	2.448
10	11.266	11.533	(.267)	.173	2.008

*Principal portion only—interest included in expenses.

Health Care

Let's now review MBIA's health care bonds. No health care issues are natural Triple-A's. (Harvard and Yale's medical schools have hospitals but they are financed with university backing). Many observers are deeply concerned over the risks they believe health care issues contain. No doubt, part of the fear arises from galloping health care costs, which in recent years have surpassed the inflation rate. Under severe economic stress, this trend might be broken. Or, revolutionary changes in the industry could significantly affect the economic landscape.

However, health care is an essential service and has performed very well financially in recessions and the Great Depression. For example, in the Depression, total medical care expenses increased as a percent of personal income, while dollars spent dropped 32.4 percent between 1929 and 1933. At the same time, hospital revenues declined only 9.9 percent (see Table 6–9). Of course, we must remember that GNP and personal income had fallen about 50 percent in the same 50-month period. Moreover, in post-World War II recessions, medical care expenditures performed largely as they did in the Great Depression, crowding out more discretionary items.

TABLE 6–9
Depression-Era Changes in Overall Medical Care Expenditures/ Hospital Revenues

Year	*Overall Medical Care Expenditures % Change from Prior Year*	*Hospital Revenues % Change from Prior Year*
1929	Base year	Base year
1930	−3.4	No change
1931	−10.1	−2.2
1932	−16.6	−2.3
1933	−6.7	−6.0
1934	+9.1	+1.7
1935	+5.7	+10.0
1936	+9.0	+3.9
1937	+7.2	+7.6
1938	+0.6	+2.9

Source: U.S. Bureau of the Census (1975).

MBIA's health care portfolio consists of 2,743 individual bond issues for 593 hospital issuers. The sector's total insured net par outstanding at year-end 1991 was $17.5 billion, and total debt service was $38.6 billion. The insured bonds consist of nonprofit hospital chains as well as single-site facilities. MBIA has sought out the top one or two hospitals in areas where it has insured an issue and has required strong management and financial performance in bonds approved for insurance.

Because health care bonds are somewhat controversial and are perceived as riskier than other, more traditional municipal bonds, we made certain our stress test was very conservative. So even though hospital revenues fell off less than 10 percent from peak to trough in the Great Depression, the test will use the more conservative performance for overall medical care expenditures to project revenues throughout the test.

Since no information is available on hospital operating expenses during the Great Depression, we needed to find a method of estimating them. We reasoned that expenses probably tracked revenues and that if a depression were to occur today, the same trend should be expected. Lending credence to this belief, Depression data indicate that the number of hospital institutions declined from 1930 through 1938, but the number of beds increased every year. This suggests that the industry consolidated, with surviving institutions growing larger and probably becoming more cost efficient. See Table 6–10.

TABLE 6–10
Depression-Era Hospital Facilities and Bed Space

Year	*Total Number of Hospitals*	*% Change from Prior Year*	*Total Number Hospital Beds (000s)*	*% Change from Prior Year*
1929	6665	Base year	907.1	Base year
1930	6719	+0.8	955.9	+5.4
1931	6613	−1.6	974.1	+1.9
1932	6562	−0.8	1014.4	+4.1
1933	6437	−1.9	1027.0	+1.2
1934	6334	−1.6	1048.1	+2.1
1935	6246	−1.4	1075.1	+2.6
1936	6189	−0.9	1096.7	+2.0
1937	6128	−1.0	1124.5	+2.5
1938	6166	+0.6	1161.4	+3.3

Source: U.S. Bureau of the Census (1975).

In this context, it would be unrealistic to assume that expenses remained constant. At the same time, we want to err on the conservative side and avoid showing a big drop-off in expenses, in order to maintain heavy stress on these issues. Therefore, we again consulted the hospital revenue statistics. From 1930 to 1933, the compound growth rate was a negative 3.4 percent and 1930 was almost level with 1929. For our model, let's presume that in the first two years expenses remain level, and for the next four, they drop at a rate of 1.7 percent, or half the actual Depression performance in revenues. For years seven to 10, for the sake of conservatism, expenses will return to year one and two levels. This combination of greater than actual revenue declines and a minuscule drop in expenses should create an ultraconservative test. In addition, as with colleges and universities, we will also presume that insured hospitals would not be able to float any new debt.

Data for the test on MBIA's hospital issues were obtained from 260 issuers or 43.8 percent of the 593 issuers in the total portfolio. The sample's key financial attributes are current-year revenues of $41.4 billion; current-year expenses of $35.9 billion; incoming cash balances (including both unrestricted and debt service reserve funds) of $13.6 billion; and debt outstanding of $17.1 billion (including other debt not insured by MBIA).

For five years, the hospital issues run deficits finally resulting in a negative cash and reserve fund balance of $240 million in year eight, the default amount. The estimated average annual principal and interest due on these issues is $1.506 billion, yielding a default ratio of 15.9 percent. To add perspective, Standard & Poor's projected Depression default rate (capital charge) for a single-site hospital is 30 percent, and for a hospital system, 20 percent, while Moody's is 15 percent for an A-rated (the typical underlying quality of an insured bond) hospital. Extrapolating this result to MBIA's total health care portfolio, we see $244.7 million defaulting in year eight—that's 15.9 percent of $1.539 billion in health care debt service. Of the 260 issuers, 39 develop defaults, most very minor. See Table 6–11.

Utilities

Utilities make up the second-largest portion of MBIA's insured bond portfolio, representing $17.8 billion of net par value and $40.2 billion of debt service outstanding as of year-end 1991. About $15.3 billion of par value is composed of municipally owned water, sewer, and electric facilities with a few solid waste operations. The remaining $2.5 billion of par value consists of investor-owned utility bonds. Like health care issuers, municipal utility bond issuers include no natural Triple-A's with which to make a comparison Similarly, only one investor-owned electric utility has a natural Triple-A.

TABLE 6–11
Depression Stress Test of MBIA Health Care (Hospital) Bonds ($ Billions)

Year	*Revenues*	*Expenses*	*Surplus (Deficit)*	*Estimatea Annual Debt Service**	*Resulting Cumulative Cash and Reserve Fund Balances*
1	$41.4	$35.9	$5.5	$0.659	$18.4
2	39.9	35.9	4.0	0.706	21.7
3	35.6	35.3	0.3	0.690	21.3
4	30.0	34.7	(4.7)	0.721	15.9
5	28.0	34.1	(6.1)	0.690	9.1
6	30.5	33.5	(3.0)	0.683	5.4
7	32.3	35.9	(3.6)	0.675	1.1
8	35.2	35.9	(0.7)	0.683	−0.24
9	37.7	35.9	1.8	0.667	0.9
10	37.9	35.9	2.0	0.651	2.2

*Principal portion only—interest is included in expenses.

Utility bonds have a superb credit record. Since the Great Depression, only three major investor-owned utilities have gone bankrupt: Public Service of New Hampshire, El Paso Electric, and Columbia Gas System. On the municipal side, Washington Public Power Supply System Projects 4 and 5 defaulted in 1983 and have the dubious distinction of being the largest municipal bond default ever, the only significant blight on an otherwise exceptionally creditworthy sector. All four of these failures had two common flaws. First was a commitment to projects beyond the issuer's financial means. The second fatal defect was long-term planning done in one economic climate, which led to overcommitment to fuel supplies or generating methods that proved unworkable in another economic environment.

Having drawn attention to these aberrations, it's important to emphasize that industry failures were by far in the minority and largely predictable long before they actually happened.

Evidence of utility bond safety abounds. In the Great Depression, investor-owned utility bonds had the best default record of any type of corporate bond. Citizens paid their utility bills with, or even before, their taxes for fear of losing electricity or water service. One indicator of utility strength was the fact that consumer utility expenditures, as part of personal consumption, rose not only as a share of personal income, but also in aggregate dollars.

According to the U.S. Bureau of the Census, the electric and water utility industries continued making profits (with the exception of 1930 for the electric utility industry) throughout the Depression. However, many companies ran operating deficits. In addition, while industry revenues went up initially, they began falling in 1932 and continued declining through 1934 (see Table 6–12). Among both electric and water utilities, small units incurred deficits while the larger ones generated profits, lending credence to size and the economies of scale as safety factors.

Hard data on utility expenses in the Depression are not readily available. However, tax-return data from the Census Bureau permit a very close approximation. It appears that from year-end 1929 through 1934, industry expenses shrank 1.8 percent per year and then grew 2.2 percent annually throughout the Depression. For extra conservatism, we will presume expenses remain level for years one to six and then begin growing 2.2 percent annually per year for years seven to 10.

We should also recall that utilities had access to the debt market in the Depression. Because of the industry's essential nature we could pre-

TABLE 6–12
Combined Electric and Water Utility Industry Revenue Performance

Year	*Percent Change in Revenues from Prior Year*
1929	Base year
1930	+5.6%
1931	No change
1932	−8.4
1933	−8.2
1934	−1.1
1935	+6.2
1936	+5.4
1937	+4.4
1938	+0.4

Source: U.S. Bureau of the Census (1930, 1940, 1975).

sume they would have the same access if a depression were to occur today. Between 1929 and 1938, public utility debt outstanding grew at a compound annual rate of 0.8 percent.[3] However, to be conservative, we will presume that outstanding debt does not increase.

We gathered data for the test from 134 issuers, or 12.6 percent of the 1,062 utility issuers MBIA has insured. However, given the sample's composition, it should at least reliably map performance under stress; it may even generate a very liberal estimate of probable defaults. The issues' key financial attributes are current year revenues of $2.31 billion; current year expenses of $2.26 billion; incoming cash balances (including both restricted and unrestricted funds) of $3.31 billion; and debt outstanding of $6.9 billion (including other debt not insured by MBIA).

Utilities finished the test with cumulative deficits in the cash balances (defaults) of $244 million year in year 10. Their estimated average annual principal and interest debt service for the sample is $703.9 million, and the total defaulting amount equals 34.7 percent of average annual debt service ($244 million divided by $703.9 million). See Table 6–13. This is high for a utility portfolio, from both a rating-agency perspective and from actual Depression experience. Default severity is apparently due largely to our ultraconservative assumptions and the possibility we extracted a sample of lower-rated issues from MBIA's portfolio.

To make a point, 77 of the 134 issuers had some defaults, though most were very minor. Standard & Poor's has a capital charge for a mu-

TABLE 6–13
Depression Stress Test of MBIA Utility Bonds ($ Billions)

Year	*Revenues*	*Expenses*	*Surplus (Deficit)*	*Estimated Annual Debt Service**	*Resulting Cumulative Cash Balance*
1	$2.310	$2.260	$0.050	$.287	$3.073
2	2.440	2.260	0.180	.310	2.943
3	2.440	2.260	0.180	.301	2.822
4	2.230	2.260	0.030	.305	2.487
5	2.050	2.260	(0.210)	.313	1.964
6	2.030	2.260	(0.230)	.323	1.411
7	2.150	2.310	(0.160)	.323	.928
8	2.270	2.360	(0.091)	.323	.514
9	2.370	2.402	(0.042)	.313	.159
10	2.380	2.466	(0.086)	.317	(.244)

*Principal portion only—interest is included in expenses.

nicipal utility set at 12 percent, but it does assess up to 40 percent for a public power agency that has substantial nuclear or project exposure. MBIA's book is predominantly water, sewer, and electric municipal utilities, with only slight exposure to nuclear plants. Moody's capital charges on utilities range from 3 percent to 34 percent, again suggesting the model projected a too-conservative default picture. Nonetheless, we will use it for our analysis.

Extrapolating the model findings into MBIA's entire book of utilities results in projected defaults of $579.9 million in year 10 (34.7 percent of $1.723 billion utility debt service in year 10).

Other Special Revenue and Structured Finance

MBIA's two remaining sectors are special revenue issues, other than colleges and universities, and housing and structured finance. For both, due to incomplete cash flow information and their small share of MBIA's total exposure, we propose using S&P's capital-charge models to determine probable defaults, which we believe will yield very conservative assumptions.

To that point, let's first review the housing and structured finance issues. Of the $7.2 billion of net par outstanding at year-end 1991, about $2.8 billion consisted of issues backed by an FHA guarantee, which theoretically includes no credit risk, only timing in collecting from the U.S.

Treasury. Another $1.2 billion of par value represented asset-backed securities where S&P computed a capital charge, or probable default rate, of 9.5 percent. The balance, or $3.2 billion in par value, consisted of such issues as state housing agencies, whose capital charges range from six percent to 20 percent. Let's presume the $3.2 billion has a 20 percent capital charge. A weighted average capital charge on the overall business would be 10.5 percent. In summary:

$2.8 billion—FHA issues	0% capital charge
$1.2 billion—asset-backed tailored charges	9.5% capital charge
$3.2 billion—all other	20% capital charge
Weighted average	10.5% capital charge

This means that the probable default on the portfolio is 10.5 percent in total of the average annual debt service. S&P also presumes the cumulative 10.5 percent default rate will occur in a specific pattern, with defaults increasing most dramatically in the third year and then doubling in the fourth year, as shown in Table 6–14. Table 6–15 projects the amount of monetary defaults at a total of $115.29 million.

MBIA's last category of insured exposure is its special revenue business that is not related to higher education. It consists generally of airport, toll road, parking, bridge, and port financings for state and local government issuers. S&P views the category as moderate to higher risk. Capital charges range from 10 percent for a limited tax-backed airport all the way to 35 percent for a toll bridge with less than five years of operating his-

TABLE 6–14
Standard & Poor's Depression Default Pattern for 10.5% Capital Charge

Year of Depression	*% of Cumulative 10.5% Default Occurring in Each Year*	*% Default/ Year*	*Cumulative % of Default*
1st	7%	0.7%	0.7%
2nd	11	1.2	1.9
3rd	30	3.2	5.1
4th	52	5.4	10.5
Total	100%	10.5%	—

Source: Standard & Poor's publications.

TABLE 6–15
Depression Stress Test of Projected Defaults for MBIA Housing/ Structured Finance Bonds ($ Millions)

Default Year	*Total Insured Debt Service/Year*	*% Default/Year*	*Projected Defaulting Debt Service/Year*
1	$1,173	0.7%	$8.21
2	1,120	1.2	13.44
3	1,080	3.2	34.56
4	1,094	5.4	59.08
Total	$4,467	10.5%	$115.29

tory. Moody's charges for this category range from 8 percent for Aaa-rated obligations to 35 percent for a Baa. For our test, we will use the worst case of 35 percent for the entire exposure, which clearly over-penalizes MBIA but also provides an ultraconservative assumption. Timing and distribution of projected defaults are the same as for housing and structured finance. Table 6–16 tabulates the defaulting amount of debt service at a total of $205.56 million.

We have now subjected all of MBIA's insured portfolio to the Depression test using conservative principles. Table 6–17 presents the sum and timing of projected Depression level defaults that might occur in the MBIA portfolio, should the Great Depression recur, or an equal cataclysm strike.

TABLE 6–16
Depression Stress Test of Projected Defaults of MBIA-Other Special Revenue Bonds ($ Millions)

Default Year	*Total Insured Debt Service/Year*	*% of Cumulative 35% Default Occurring/Year*	*% Default/ Year*	*Projected Defaulting Debt Service/Year*
1	$541	7%	2.4%	$12.98
2	607	11	3.9	23.67
3	586	30	10.5	61.53
4	590	52	5.4	107.38
Total	$2,324	100%	35.0%	$205.56

TABLE 6–17

Depression Stress Test Summary of MBIA—All Insured Bond Sectors/Projected Defaulting Debt Service by Year

($ Millions)

Year	*Tax-Backed and G.O.'s*	*Higher Education*	*Health Care*	*Utilities*	*Housing/ Structured Finance*	*Other Special Revenue*	*Total*
1	—	—	—	—	$8.21	$12.98	$ 21.19
2	—	—	—	—	13.44	23.67	37.11
3	—	—	—	—	34.56	61.53	96.09
4	—	—	—	—	59.08	107.38	166.46
5	—	—	—	—	—	—	—
6	$115.40	—	—	—	—		115.40
7	—	—	—	—	—	—	—
8	—	—	$244.70	—	—	—	244.70
9	—	—	—	—	—	—	—
10	—	—	—	$597.90	—	—	597.90
Total	$115.40	—	$244.70	$597.90	$115.29	$205.56	$1,278.85

ASSET STRESS

Throughout the 10-year cycle of our simulated depression, the demands on MBIA's resources total almost $1.3 billion. We must now see how MBIA assets will meet this level of stress.

To meet any potential obligations, MBIA's balance sheet as of year-end 1991 showed assets of almost $2.3 billion, liabilities of $1.2 billion, and net worth of slightly over $1 billion. In addition, MBIA's annual report describes supplemental standby credit facilities with a total of four major banks for a total of $575 million:

> MBIA Corp. has a standby line of credit commitment in the amount of $500 million with a major bank to provide loans to MBIA Corp. after it has incurred cumulative losses (net of any recoveries) from December 31, 1991, in excess of the greater of $450 million and 6.25% of average annual debt service. The obligation to repay loans made under this agreement is a limited recourse obligation, payable solely from, and collateralized by, a pledge of recoveries realized on defaulted insured obligations including certain installment premiums and other collateral. This commitment has a seven-year term and expires on December 31, 1998, but, subject to approval by the bank, may be annually renewed to extend the term to seven years beyond the renewal date.
>
> MBIA Corp. also has committed short-term lines of credit for claims-paying purposes aggregating $75 million with three other major banks.[4]

Let's now look more critically at available assets to determine how they would be likely to perform in another Great Depression. Table 6–18 is the company's Consolidated Balance Sheet as of December 31, 1991. Among MBIA's consolidated balance sheet items are deferred acquisition costs, goodwill, property and equipment, and other assets. These are either intangible assets or ones that would probably be illiquid in a depression, and therefore of no value to bondholders. On the liability side, since insured bondholders would have first claim, holding company debtholders and other liability claims would be in a subordinated position, and would not reduce assets needed for claims. Unearned premiums are an offset to cash received for premium and likewise would not restrict an asset's use. Deferred taxes result mostly from timing differences between the Statutory (Regulatory) and GAAP (Generally Accepted Accounting Principles) accounting methods; in a depression they probably would not become due because of operating losses that would offset them. The loss

TABLE 6–18
Consolidated Balance Sheets

Dollars in Thousands except per Share Amounts	*December 31, 1991*
Assets	
Investments:	
Fixed maturity securities, at amortized cost (market value $1,939,130 and $1,650,908)	$1,842,271
Short-term investments, at amortized cost (which approximates market value)	93,100
Other investments	26,010
Total investments	1,961,381
Cash and cash equivalents	4,427
Accrued investment income	37,670
Deferred acquisition costs	97,173
Goodwill (less accumulated amortization of $20,857 and $15,372)	126,502
Property and equipment, at cost (less accumulated depreciation of $5,696 and $3,807)	33,480
Receivable for investments sold	2,379
Other assets	15,375
Total assets	$2,278,387
Liabilities and Shareholders' Equity	
Liabilities:	
Unearned premiums	$ 858,544
Loss and loss adjustment expense reserve	21,173
Long-term debt	198,692
Current income taxes payable	—
Deferred income taxes	87,967
Other liabilities	48,674
Total liabilities	1,215,050
Commitments and Contingencies	
Shareholders' Equity	
Preferred stock, par value $1 per share; authorized shares—10,000,000; issued and outstanding—none	—
Common stock, par value $1 per share; authorized shares—100,000,000; issued shares—39,030,112	39,030
Additional paid-in capital	567,505
Retained earnings	468,531
Cumulative translation adjustment	(133)
Unrealized appreciation (depreciation) of investments, net of deferred income taxes of $82 in 1991	159
Treasury stock, at cost; 474,544 shares in 1991 and 761,453 shares in 1990	(11,755)
Total shareholders' equity	1,063,337
Total liabilities and shareholders' equity	$2,278,387

and adjustment expense reserve includes actual claims in default or potential defaults, and should be subtracted from assets.

What remains? These elements: cash and equivalents and invested assets and a receivable for sold investments. The value of the cash and equivalents, short-term investments, and the sold investment receivable should be fully available to pay claims in a depression. What about MBIA's longer term bond portfolio and other investments? By all measures, MBIA has a strong bond portfolio that should perform well under stress, as shown in Tables 6–19 and 6–20.

We reviewed what actually happened to various bond types in the Great Depression to develop a basis for the asset portfolio's stress test.

As shown in Table 6–21, we reviewed changes in bond prices per year from 1929 through 1938. These provided the means of determining the amount at which a particular bond could be liquidated, should that be necessary to meet claims payments.

For our test of MBIA's strength and ability to survive a Great Depression, we subjected the bond portfolio to changes in value found in such Depression-era patterns. MBIA's other invested assets, a portfolio of equity securities, underwent similar Depression-era conditions, as summarized in Table 6–22.

In addition to their potential liquidation value, it is important to assess the assets' cash flow or income stream. In 1991, the investment portfolio also had a core income stream from fixed maturities of $128,408,000; from short-term investments, $4,210,000; and from other investments, $1,030,000, less investment expenses of $2,010,000. That leaves a net total of $131,638,000. However, in a depression, the $1.03 million in dividend income would probably be severely curtailed. For our test, we will presume it is fully eliminated, leaving a core stream of $130,608,000. This number equates to a yield of 6.3 percent on $2,062,667,000 of earning assets (all fixed incomes, short terms, others, and cash equivalents). We will use the lower of the core stream or the percent of earning assets to project the portfolio's annual earnings during the stress test. The 6.3 percent (or core stream) is presumed to be an overall portfolio yield covering, as an average, all invested assets.

Before we test the strength of the asset portfolio and superimpose default claims upon MBIA's resources, let's recall the resources available to meet obligations: total available balance sheet resources are $2,043,873,000 after netting for current loss revenues. As the test begins, this will be the base amount available to pay claims. Invested assets will be adjusted each year for Depression-era changes in values after we have determined the proj-

TABLE 6–19
MBIA Asset Analysis/Long-Term Bond Portfolio as of 12/31/91 ($ Thousands)

Bond Type	*Amortized Cost*	*Market Value*
Taxable bonds		
United States Treasury and government agency	$295,640	$322,378
Corporate and other obligations	206,678	226,190
Tax-exempt bonds		
State and municipal obligations	1,339,953	1,390,562
Total	$1,842,271	$1,939,130

Maturity Schedule	*Amortized Cost*	*Market Value*
Beyond 1 year but within 5 years	$373,349	$383,474
Beyond 5 years but within 10 years	599,868	631,466
Beyond 10 years but within 15 years	394,519	417,382
Beyond 15 years but within 20 years	227,073	239,509
Beyond 20 years	247,462	267,299
Total	$1,842,271	$1,939,130

TABLE 6–20
MBIA Asset Analysis/Long-Term Bond Portfolio by Credit Rating as of 12/31/91

Quality Rating	*Percent of Portfolio*
Aaa	39.7%
Aa	34.7%
A	22.9%
Baa	2.7%
Total	100.0%

ected amount of Depression-test claims. If we need the letter of credit, we will project the estimated draw in the years needed. See Table 6–23.

In addition, our test will presume that MBIA ceases writing new insurance business, all premium cash flow subsides, and the company's only income is from its investment portfolio. MBIA will also have ongoing operating expenses; in 1991, they were about $47.6 million net of costs incurred to write new business. We will presume these expenses continue throughout the test, and that any cash flow is reinvested in short-term securities.

For the sake of simplicity our model also does not include income tax payments or returns. This is somewhat liberal in years one, two, five,

TABLE 6–21
Bond Price Performance in the Great Depression from 1929–1938
(Percent Change in Price from Prior Year)

Year	*U.S. Government*	*State and Local Government*	*Corporate Aaa*
1929	Base year	Base year	Base year
1930	+3.8	+2.6	+2.0
1931	−14.7	+1.0	+2.0
1932	−4.2	−8.3	−9.1
1933	+4.7	−0.8	+8.1
1934	+2.5	+9.5	+7.7
1935	+4.3	+8.9	+7.4
1936	+1.3	+4.8	+3.9
1937	−0.7	−0.4	+0.5
1938	+1.7	+2.9	+1.4

Source: U.S. Bureau of the Census (1975).

TABLE 6–22
Great Depression Stock Market Performance (Standard & Poor's Index of Common Stocks)

Year	*Percent Change in Value from Prior Year*
1929	Base year
1930	−19.2
1931	−35.0
1932	−49.3
1933	+29.3
1934	+9.8
1935	+7.7
1936	+45.9
1937	−0.3
1938	−25.4

TABLE 6–23
MBIA Resource Summary ($ Millions)

Asset	*Amount*	*Adjustment Comments*
Cash equivalents	$ 4.427	No adjustment
Sold investment receivable	2.379	No adjustment
Short-term investments	93.100	No adjustment
Fixed maturities	1,939.130	To be adjusted for Depression-era performance
Other investments	26.010	To be adjusted for Depression-era performance
Less current loss reserves	(21.173)	No adjustment
Total available balance sheet resources	$2,043.873	—
Plus letter of credit facilities	575.000	No adjustment
Total of all resources available at beginning of test	$2,619.873	—

seven, and nine, since MBIA does have premium earnings and investment income from taxable interest. If we presumed positive cash flow was close to taxable income, then the estimated tax due would amount to an additional $117.7 million for those years. However, losses in all of the other years overwhelm any earnings and would generate substantial returns of about $275.5 million. Therefore, leaving this item out of the model is, on balance, conservative.

In addition, the model does not make any provision for reinsurer failure. At year-end 1991, MBIA had ceded $31.5 billion of principal and interest risk to reinsurers. The default rate on MBIA's retained business is 0.7 percent, calculated by taking the $1.279 billion projected defaults and dividing by total net MBIA exposure of $184.6 billion at year-end 1991. If we assume that reinsured risk defaulted in the same pattern as MBIA's retained business, then the total default rate on reinsured debt service would be $220.5 million (.007 times $31.5 billion). Even if every reinsurer failed to pay every dime owed, MBIA would still have nearly $1.7 billion in assets at the end of the depression. The more likely scenario is that most, if not all, reinsurers would pay on time.

What other problems could injure MBIA's ability to service the insured bond portfolio? What about investment income and the realizable value of invested assets MBIA would use to pay defaults? The model has adjusted these values based on Depression-era statistics. The cash and short-term assets, plus government bonds can service all cash calls until the ninth year, the second-to-last year of the test. Even if values in the corporate and tax-exempt bond portfolio are excessively optimistic, over $1.8 billion remains to be liquidated, essentially in a period of recovery. Therefore, it does not seem necessary to make further adjustments here.

In terms of yield, could a more pessimistic scenario be justified? First, only the fixed-income portfolio is generating income, and the cash and equivalents and government bonds should pay interest on a timely basis. Value adjustments on the corporate and tax-exempts will affect the yield, and this is reflected in our model. Here again, what if value assessments are too optimistic and yield is not realized because of defaults in the asset portfolio? Since this is a high quality portfolio, it should perform at least as well as the insured bonds, and more likely as well as the

Year of Test	*Original Projected Investment Income*	*Reciprocal of Default Factor*	*Pessimistic Estimate of Investment Income*
1	$130.6 million	.99	$129.3 million
2	130.6 million	.98	127.9 million
3	130.6 million	.95	124.1 million
4	130.6 million	.92	120.1 million
Cumulative total	$522.4 million		$501.4 million

TABLE 6–24

Depression Stress Test—MBIA Assets and Cash Flows (Projected Asset Values, Investment Income and Cash Flows per Year, $ Millions)

	Asset Categories with Projected Values at Year End						*Cash Flows*		
Year	*Cash and Short-Term Receivables*	*Government Bonds*	*Corporate Bonds*	*Tax-Exempt Bonds*	*Other Investments*	*Year-End Total Value*	*Investment Income*	*Less Operating Expenses*	*Less Defaults*
Value at test inception	78.7*	$322.4	$226.2	$1,390.6	$26.0	$2,043.9	$130.6	$47.6	N/A
1	140.5	322.4	226.2	1390.6	26.0	2105.7	130.6	47.6	21.19
2	186.4	334.7	230.7	1426.8	21.0	2199.6	130.6	47.6	37.11
3	173.3	285.5	235.3	1441.1	13.7	2148.9	130.6	47.6	96.09
4	89.8	273.5	213.9	1321.5	6.9	1905.6	130.6	47.6	166.46
5	162.2	286.4	231.2	1310.9	8.9	1999.6	120.0	47.6	—
6	125.2	293.5	249.0	1435.4	9.8	2113.0	126.0	47.6	115.4
7	208.2	306.1	267.4	1563.2	10.6	2355.6	130.6	47.6	—
8	46.5	310.1	277.9	1638.2	15.5	2288.2	130.6	47.6	244.7
9	129.5	307.9	279.3	1631.6	15.5	2363.8	130.6	47.6	200.6
10			204.6	1678.9	11.6	1895.1	130.6	47.6	597.7

*Presumes current loss reserves have been deducted from this category at inception of test.

natural Triple-A's. However, to be clearly conservative, let's presume the asset portfolio suffers a 16 percent cumulative default rate, in keeping with S&P's model, and that this produces lower realized yields in the first four test years as shown on the Table on page 97.

In those four years, cash flow from investment income slips by $21 million, not enough to affect the test's overall outcome.

Summary

Let's now sum up the total results of the stress test. Table 6–24 presents asset values by category, cash flows, expenses, and defaults for each test year and adjusts the value of the assets for Depression-era performance.

What is the test's bottom line? MBIA makes it through a Great Depression scenario intact with the ability to meet all of its obligations. It does not generate sufficient losses to require tapping its letter of credit facility. Moreover, not only could MBIA pay its insured bondholders, but it could also meet interest obligations on its parent company debt on a cash-flow basis, and it concludes the period with a $1.9 billion asset portfolio.

Natural Triple-A's do not fare quite as well. While the higher educational institutions are solid, the tax-backed and general obligation portfolio develops small defaults in year six of the test. It is clear that two forms of protection—a fundamentally good underlying bond issue and the extra layer of protection provided by insurance—serve the bondholder well.

NOTES

1. Robert R. Godfrey, *Risk Based Capital Charges for Municipal Bonds*, (Greenwich: JAI Press Inc., 1990); and Bond Investors Association.
2. George H. Hempel, *The Postwar Quality of State and Local Debt*, National Bureau of Economic Research (New York: Columbia University Press, 1971).
3. W. Braddock Hickman, *The Volume of Corporate Bond Financing Since 1900*, National Bureau of Economic Research (Princeton, NJ: Princeton University Press, 1953).
4. MBIA Inc. Annual Report, 1991, p. 37.

CHAPTER 7

MARKETABILITY: COMPARING NATURAL TRIPLE-A'S TO INSURED BONDS

To this point we have concentrated on default risk, trying to determine whether significant credit quality differences exist between natural and insured Triple-A bonds. Now it's time to examine marketability and its effect on trading value.

As Larry Hastie pointed out in his 1972 study, "Determinants of Municipal Bond Yields,"

> Marketability is concerned with the price that buyers pay and sellers receive when they wish to alter their holdings. If an investor is certain that he will not need to liquidate his investment prior to maturity, he is not concerned with marketability. Or, if the market for municipal bonds were perfect or highly efficient, marketability would be of no concern. However, because the principal investors in the municipal bond market do have a potential need to liquidate their holdings prior to maturity and because the market is not highly efficient, marketability may be an important determinant of municipal yields. There are three types of measures that are relevant for assessing the marketability of a municipality's bonds: measures of *block marketability*, measures of *issuer marketability*, and measures that predict *future marketability*.[1] (emphasis added)

Even though the complexion and size of the market have changed significantly in the past two decades, Hastie's measures still seem logical and should be tested today. In addition, we searched for our own indicator of relative demand for bonds, or marketability, and found the *placement ratio* as a proxy, which we will explore later in this chapter.

BLOCK MARKETABILITY

Hastie's first point was that a larger block of bonds would tend to be more marketable than a smaller one because a core amount of analysis, at a cost, must be done before a purchase is made. Let's evaluate his premise.

The 141 natural Triple-A issuers in 1991 have the advantage of being a small group to examine with an average issue size of $84 million. In 1991, the average insured issue size was $20 million. However, it could just as easily be argued that since the bond insurers stand in the shoes of the issuer, the market has only five major bond insurers to analyze versus 141 separate natural Triple-A's. If buyers review both the insurer and issuer, the premise loses some validity because the investor is looking through the insurer to the underlying issuer. In this sense, naturals do have the advantage of larger initial block size, but 10 basis points of interest rate spread (1991's lowest appropriate monthly yield differential) translates into $1 in interest per $1000 bond per year. The $64 million difference in block size penalizes the insured Triple-A $64,000 each year in additional interest.

Logic suggests that the additional yield on the insured bond compensates its holders many times for the variation in block size. It simply should not cost the bond buyer $64,000 a year to do the analysis. In addition, Hastie found that block size increases from $5,000 to $50,000 had significant effects, but increases from $200,000 to $300,000 had little effect. Even with the inflation of the last 20 years, the $20 million average issue has certainly reached the threshold block size, making the yield penalty unwarranted.

ISSUER MARKETABILITY

Hastie says,

> The marketability of an issuer is usually discussed in terms of the thinness of the market for *that particular issue*. One measure of issuer marketability might be the size of the issuer's net debt outstanding. The argument used to support net debt outstanding as a good measure of marketability is the following: all other things being equal, the smaller the number of bonds outstanding, the fewer the transactions we should expect to take place; the less fre-

> quently transactions occur, the thinner the market; the thinner the market, the more uncertain the price and the less marketable the issuer's bonds. This view of marketability suggests that bonds of frequent issuers of debt are more marketable than bonds of issuers with little debt outstanding. On the other hand, some investors tend to view the marketability of an issuer's bonds as it relates to their own portfolios. If a specific issuer already represents a significant portion of an investor's portfolio, the issue may be acceptable only if the yields rise relative to the rest of the market. This view suggests that the yields of larger issuers may be higher than those of otherwise comparable issuers; it suggests that the bonds of smaller issuers may be more marketable than those of larger issuers.[2]

Following this logic, insured bonds have an overwhelming advantage in issue size since they are the bulk of the total Triple-A market. However, because of their size, insured bonds are penalized for their abundance.

Hastie's research tends to confirm that when individuals dominate the market, they extract a yield premium when an issuer has a large debt. Let us apply more current analysis and perspective. Again, the analytical techniques and methods of bond buyers are important. If investors are analyzing both the bond issuer and the insurer, then insured bonds could be penalized in yield for smaller block size per issue. They would suffer again from the large number of insured bonds outstanding if the buyer believes that scarcity (smaller amounts of debt) holds down yields.

The numbers need perspective. Using 1991 new issue volume as the indicator, we will assume that buyers penalized insured bonds for being too plentiful. Natural Triple-A issues totaled about $10 billion, while insured issues hit almost $52 billion. With the 10 basis points of interest-rate differential, 1991 buyers extracted $52 million in additional annual interest because the issues had a larger debt volume. This number seems completely out of proportion since the amount of insured volume increases liquidity and facilitates trading. Moreover, evidence suggests that bond investors are relying heavily on the insurance alone. Consider the performance of Philadelphia bonds (insured and uninsured) during the city's 1990 financial crisis. Uninsured bonds lost 13.8 percent of their value while insured bonds actually rose slightly in value, indicating that bond holders and buyers rely on the insurer's strength instead of the issuer's. Besides protecting prices, bond insurance adds value, as the prices of New York City bonds showed in 1991–92. See Tables 7–1 and 7–2.

TABLE 7–1
Price Protection of Bond Insurance
Price of Philadelphia General Obligation Bonds, ($1,000,000 Par Value)

	Uninsured Bonds	*MBIA-Insured Bonds*
April 6, 1990	$993,650	$1,020,210
December 28, 1990	856,140	1,026,190
Change in value	($137,510)	$ 5,980
Percent change	−13.8%	+0.5%

TABLE 7–2
Added Value of Bond Insurance
Price of New York State General Obligation Bonds, ($1,000,000 Par Value)

	Uninsured Bonds	*MBIA-Insured Bonds*
March 14, 1991	$861,170	$878,710
January 16, 1992	916,690	964,640
Change in value	$ 55,520	$ 85,930
Percent change	+6.4%	+9.8%

FUTURE ISSUER MARKETABILITY

Hastie points out,

> If an investor does not expect to sell his bonds immediately, he is more interested in future than in present marketability. If the current total debt is a measure of current marketabililty, then future total debt should be a measure of future marketability. Since the local citizenry determines which facilities and services are required, the future demands of the residents would be an indicator of future debt outstanding. One possible measure of future demands is past population growth. Past population growth is preferred to current population growth, because it is a better estimate of the changing demand for capital expenditures—the major use of borrowed capital. As the population grows, so do the demands for schools, roads, and other public services requiring large capital outlays, but these demands tend to lag behind actual changes in population. These capital outlays are usually made only after existing facilities have become overcrowded and the citizenry has expressed its demands. For these reasons, past population

> growth appears to be the best measure of future demands for capital expenditures, and, in turn, for future increases in debt.
>
> As in the case of current issuer marketability, future marketability can be discussed from two apparently conflicting viewpoints. According to one argument, an increase in total debt would increase the amount of the issuer's bonds relative to the total market, thereby impairing the bond's marketability. The two views of issuer marketability tend to suggest opposite conclusions regarding the effect of current and future debt outstanding. If the empirical results are to be meaningful, they should confirm the validity of one of these two views.[3]

Hastie found that faster growing communities did suffer a yield penalty because the market saw a future oversupply. A review of the natural Triple-A's, MBIA's portfolio, and national statistics seems in order. From 1980 to 1990, the naturals had a compound annual population growth rate of 1.18 percent. MBIA's book of tax-backed issuers averaged 1.5 percent, and countrywide annual growth was .94 percent. While the insured bond group definitely grew fastest, all three sectors actually had anemic growth rates. And, although insured bonds grew fastest, they benefited from the added security of the insurance, which should have reduced the yield penalty.

THE PLACEMENT RATIO

To apply a new insight into marketability, we sought a measure that might irrefutably confirm why one bond is more desirable than another. We settled on the competitive placement ratio as a surrogate for investor demand for different types of bonds.

The placement ratio is a yardstick that measures investors' interest in new tax-exempt issuers in any given week. While the formula has varied slightly over the years, it generally resembles the one used today. Calculating the placement ratio involves only issues of $10 million or greater par value that come to market through a competitive sale. The ratio is the amount of par sold by the end of the offering week, divided by the original par available. The higher the ratio, the fewer bonds left in the account. Since it is only calculated on competitive sales of $10 million or more, the placement ratio usually represents less than 20 percent of total municipal new issue business. Nonetheless, the ratio can be a valuable barometer of demand and may provide insights into value differences.

Key influences on the placement ratio are the supply-demand balance, expectations of interest-rate movement, and the competitive pressure from any inventory backlog. Since these factors interact in many ways to influence the placement ratio, we cannot predict how each one might affect it. For instance, low volume (30-day visible supply) might be the catalyst for a high placement ratio. However, if the low volume was caused by rapidly rising rates, investors might be waiting for the market to settle, causing instead a low placement ratio.

Investor perceptions of default risk and the marketability of the issues selling in a given week also affect the ratio. This allows us to suggest the placement ratio as a proxy for measuring the quality of new bonds the market sees in any one week. Further, if the natural Triple-A bonds and the insured Triple-A bonds are set out in discrete market segments, the placement ratio may have something to teach us about these two bond groups.

The ratios for the whole market, the natural Triple-A, and the insured Triple-A's for the years 1989, 1990, and 1991 are summarized in Table 7–3, and have been statistically refined and graphed in Figure 7–1. We should point out that in this chapter, insured data include all insured bonds by all municipal bond guarantors, not just MBIA.

While no pattern emerges immediately, the regression graph (Figure 7–1) shows that the natural Triple-A market has a higher overall ratio, as might be expected, and the ratio has increased over time. Insured bonds, on the other hand, were at a slightly lower level and remained flat through the three-year period. The overall market rises slightly, and all three segments show very good placement results.

Since volume influences the placement ratio, we need to examine the par issued in each sector to see if any explanation emerges. First, the long-term municipal market grew 17.5 percent a year, increasing from \$124.9 billion to \$172.6 billion. At the same time, the insured market grew 33.2 percent, from \$29.1 billion to \$51.7 billion, a rate almost double the total market. Natural Triple-A issuance rose from \$5.4 billion to \$9.9 billion, a 35.9 percent annual rate, even faster than the insured market.

However, growth rates do not tell the complete story. In 1989, insured bonds accounted for 23.2 percent of the total market and grew to 29.9 percent of a larger market in 1991. Naturals had 4.3 percent of the 1989 market and increased to only 5.7 percent of the 1991 market. Naturals started from a relatively small base and remained low. During those

TABLE 7–3
Municipal Bond Placement Ratio (%)

Period	*Total Market*	*Natural Triple A's*	*Insured Market*
January 89	82.8	71.2	87.9
February 89	78.6	97.0	83.4
March 89	80.5	69.0	58.8
April 89	90.2	94.5	91.4
May 89	83.7	85.2	86.0
June 89	81.0	83.9	76.6
July 89	78.1	87.1	70.9
August 89	76.9	63.7	74.5
September 89	83.1	82.4	80.1
October 89	76.9	100.0	76.1
November 89	86.8	76.6	68.0
December 89	75.1	66.4	78.7
January 90	85.5	97.6	69.3
February 90	85.9	81.9	91.6
March 90	75.5	85.0	73.2
April 90	82.8	84.7	74.3
May 90	89.6	100.0	81.4
June 90	82.5	83.9	73.6
July 90	84.1	100.0	78.1
August 90	93.0	99.4	91.7
September 90	88.0	94.2	83.7
October 90	90.7	88.6	86.7
November 90	79.9	93.7	76.9
December 90	72.2	90.7	63.8
January 91	85.9	N/A	85.4
February 91	73.2	68.1	82.3
March 91	77.8	82.5	78.2
April 91	83.5	96.4	83.2
May 91	89.6	77.7	83.6
June 91	83.0	90.7	80.8
July 91	87.1	94.3	70.8
August 91	89.3	100.0	83.2
September 91	87.5	89.9	66.8
October 91	78.9	87.2	80.5
November 91	84.1	77.6	70.9
December 91	95.4	93.9	91.0

Source: Bond Buyer/MBIA Database.

three years, State of California issues comprised a large percentage of the natural Triple-A par issued. Without California, the natural market had no growth, and anecdotal evidence suggests California paid a premium in yield over other naturals, such as State of North Carolina and Westchester

FIGURE 7–1
Competitive Placement Ratio Trend*

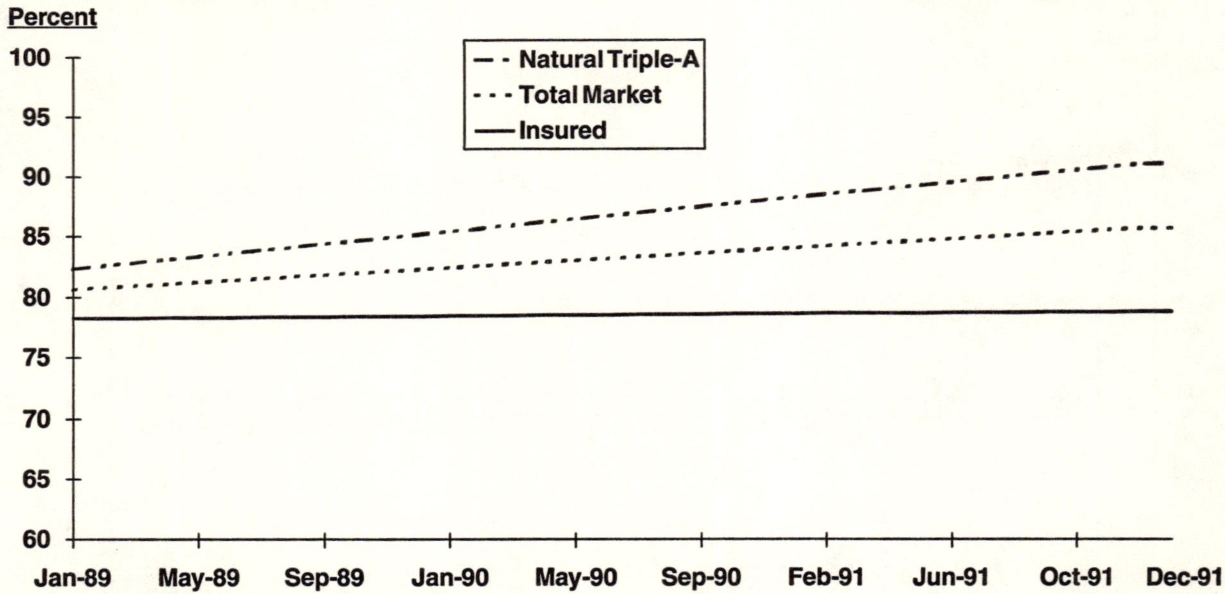

*Competitive Issues of $10 million or greater par value.

County, New York, to get its bonds sold. Specifically, on September 25, 1991, a California issue with 10-year maturities paid an eye-popping 25 basis points more in yield than a comparable North Carolina issue.

A central lesson: Supply and demand largely determine the pace at which bonds get placed. The large increase in the already large insured sector might have weakened the market's ability to absorb more insured issues. However, the insured market maintained a very respectable placement ratio even as it increased its share of the total market. This documents the value that investors recognize in buying an Aaa/AAA bond, but one with greater yield. In addition, the chicken-or-the-egg argument emerges. Presumably, the insured bond supply would not have grown without buyer demand. If so, market indigestion is not an adequate explanation, yet we are confronted with the fact that during the three-year period, insured bonds were not snapped up quite as fast as other bonds.

CONCLUSIONS

In our study of bond marketability, we found the first seemingly rational explanation of the yield differentials between natural and insured Triple-A bonds. Yet, at the same time, the data leave the analyst still trying to find the rationale. Moreover, the data, at best, present an inconclusive picture with insured bonds having some advantages and natural Triple-A's having others. Furthermore, where the naturals prevail, the yield spread seems grossly out of proportion. To summarize the marketability points and attempt to formulate plausible explanations:

Block Marketability. Measured by offering size, naturals have an advantage. However, both insured bonds and naturals are well above the threshold that should conceivably make a difference. In essence, both bond groups are on a par in this category. If this were the only marketability criterion for determining trading value, insured and natural Triple-A's should trade the same.

Issuer Marketability. Here, according to conventional wisdom, when retail investors dominate the marketplace—as they have for several years—issuers are penalized for an oversupply of bonds. However, demand from retail investors has in large part stimulated the growth of insured bonds. In addition, natural Triple-A's issued $10 billion of bonds in

1991 out of a total long-term market of $173 billion. That's hardly a scarcity of issuance. Finally, the estimated $52 million yield penalty assessed from insured bonds versus natural Triple-A's more than compensates for the degrees of relative scarcity.

Future Issuer Marketability. Insured bond issuers grew faster in population than the naturals, but both groups grew more quickly than the country at large. Therefore, one must presume that both natural Triple-A's and insured issues are going to have greater future financing needs than the balance of the state and local government community. Also, while population growth rates do differ, the rates in all three sectors are absolutely anemic.

Placement Ratio. Insured bonds did not place as well as naturals or as well as the overall municipal bond market. On further examination, we saw the insured market grew faster than either the market at large or the natural Triple-A's—after we eliminated California—in terms of overall par value issued from 1989–1991. Some market indigestion could be expected with such growth rates. However, no one forced investors to buy insured bonds. Presumably, buyer demand also prompted the growth.

After sifting and digesting all the information on marketability, we can conclude that:

- Marketability is, at best, a soft concept which essentially defies hard quantitative analysis or statistical benchmarks. It is largely a matter of perception. Moreover, marketability does not exist independently of a bond's perceived default risk. The two concepts are interdependent.
- Despite bond insurance's presence in the market for 20 years, its prevalence and significance are still relatively new. It is no doubt erroneously perceived as is any other new concept. Conversely, natural Triple-A's enjoy an historically unwarranted perception of unlimited financial strength and a bottomless pool of tax and fee dollars.
- Due to the relative newness of bond insurance and the lack of understanding about it, the yield differentials between insured and natural Triple-A bonds have created a market inefficiency that allows investors to reap a windfall by purchasing and holding in-

sured bonds. On the other hand, natural Triple-A buyers are paying dearly for the myth of unlimited taxing power and financial resources. As with any inefficient market, time and knowledge should eventually close the gap.

NOTES

1. K. Larry Hastie, "Determinants of Municipal Bond Yields," *Journal of Finance and Quantitative Analysis*, June 1972, p. 1732.
2. Ibid., p. 1733.
3. Ibid., pp. 1733–34.

CHAPTER 8

LESSONS FROM OTHER BOND MARKETS

No study of trading value would be complete without an examination of the one major bond market where every issue is Triple-A and where there are large numbers of yield differentials—the U.S. government bond market. Here, we can discern parallels and perhaps gain insight into the need for more efficient marketing methods. Specifically, we will explore the history, characteristics, trading attributes, and relationships of the U.S. Treasury and government-related agencies for conclusions that may be relevant to municipal bonds. First, however, we should review some of the factors causing yield differentials in these bonds.

Part of the differential results from state income (and related) taxes many jurisdictions levy on the mortgage agencies but not on Treasury bonds. Also, the Government National Mortgage Association (GNMA) and the other housing agency pass-through securities carry a "duration penalty" because they return monthly principal and interest, unlike a Treasury bond which pays off at maturity. When interest rates rise, GNMA maturities stretch out, and, when rates fall, principal payments accelerate because of mortgage prepayments and refinancings. Generally, the market imposes a yield penalty for these developments. However, even after eliminating these effects, we find that a default risk premium exists among bonds with the same rating and, when stripped to bare essentials, nearly identical security. In the government bond market, history and recent occurrences provide many clues to yield differentials. See Figure 8–1.

Marketable debt issued by or related to the U.S. government takes many forms. Direct debt, issued by the U.S. Treasury, is secured by the full faith and credit of the federal government. Marketable Treasury securities were first authorized by the Liberty Bond Act of September 24, 1917, and are subject to limits set by Congress. Consisting of bills, notes,

FIGURE 8–1
U.S. Treasury versus Government Mortgage Yields (30 Year)

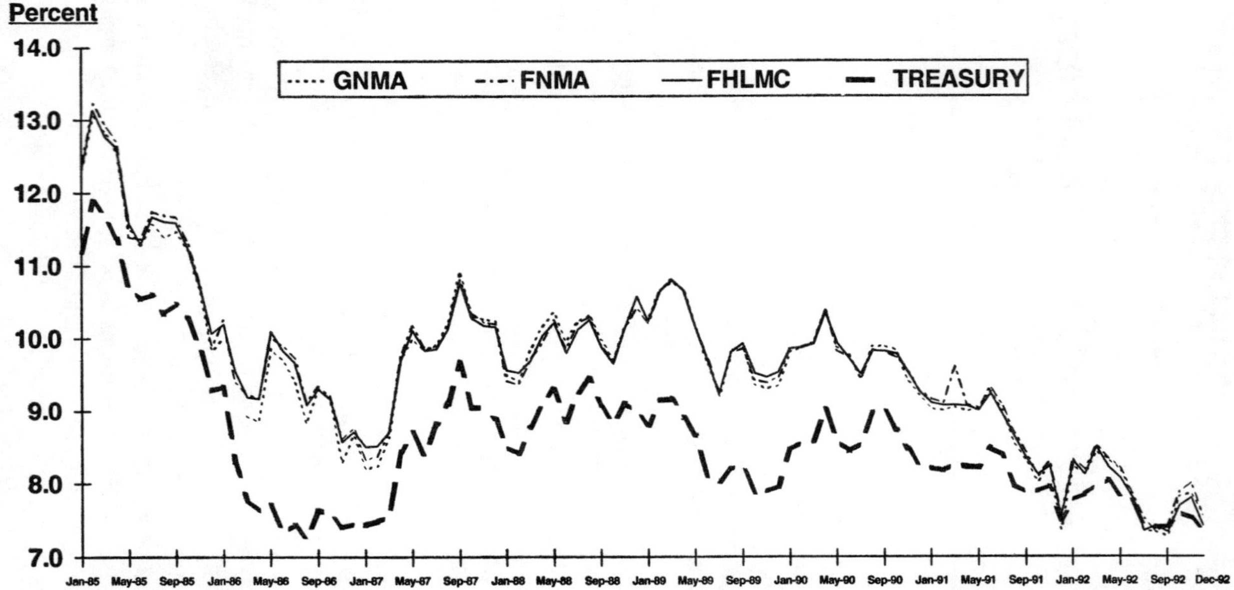

Source: Bloomberg Financial Markets; *The Bond Buyer*.

and bonds of various maturities, they are universally accepted as the safest investment available. Also issued under Congressional authority are securities of several federal agencies; some are classified as government-sponsored enterprises (GSEs). Each agency relates somewhat differently to the federal government in its ability to borrow from the Treasury, its exemption from state tax, and its ownership.

Federal agencies have evolved with the nation. The first pure government-sponsored enterprise, the Federal Land Bank, was established by Congress in 1916, the forerunner of today's Farm Credit System. As the country's agricultural credit needs expanded, the agency grew. During the Great Depression, Congress created several more agencies. The Federal Home Loan Banks came into being in 1932. They provided loans to member banks which enabled lenders to offer residential mortgages. In 1933, the Tennessee Valley Authority (TVA) was established to develop power resources in the Tennessee Valley region and to strengthen the economy and the national defense.

The 1930s also gave birth to several housing-related agencies which would eventually assume important roles in U.S. housing finance. The Federal Housing Administration (FHA) was introduced in 1934. In 1938, the Federal National Mortgage Association (FNMA, or Fannie Mae) was incorporated as part of the National Mortgage Association of Washington, which split in 1968 into FNMA and the Government National Mortgage Association (GNMA, Ginnie Mae). All were established to make affordable housing finance more available. These agencies were well entrenched in government operations when the housing market boomed after World War II. They were joined in 1970 by the Federal Home Mortgage Corp. (FHMC, Freddie Mac), which is primarily a mortgage guarantor or insurer with the same mission as the other agencies.

The need for government guarantees reached to other sectors of the economy. In 1972, the Student Loan Marketing Association (Sallie Mae) was created as a U.S. government agency. Primarily, Sallie Mae provides liquidity for banks, S&L's, and other originators of government-guaranteed student loans. By the early 1970s, the government's cost of financing these agencies and others was growing. The Federal Financing Bank (FFB) was established in 1973 to consolidate and reduce these costs by purchasing obligations issued, sold, or guaranteed by federal agencies, excluding GSEs.

From the early 1970s until the S&L debacle in the late 1980s, no new agencies that issued securities were created. Financing Corp. (FICO) and Resolution Funding Corp. (Refcorp) were established in 1987 and 1989, respectively. FICO was to recapitalize FSLIC; Refcorp was to finance Resolution Trust Corp. (RTC), which was to help the government dispose of the assets of failed thrift institutions.

Each agency has a different status with the U.S. government. Federal support is either explicit or implicit. Among those enjoying explicit full faith and credit are the Federal Financing Bank, the U.S. Maritime Administration, FHA, and GNMA. In particular, GNMA guarantees the debt of other issuers, which, in turn, is backed by the full faith and credit of the United States. Thus, GNMA securities have the safety and liquidity of Treasury securities. So strong is this security that S&P, for example, rates them as "AAA qualified instruments without reviewing the debt security or the issuer."[1]

In contrast are GSEs, which have implied U.S. government support. Although this classification has not been specially defined by law, GSEs have certain common elements. They are federally chartered to fulfill a public purpose, organized in corporate form, and linked to the federal government. This link is some form of federal backing, such as a line of credit with the U.S. Treasury. Government support implies that although the federal government does not have a legal obligation to support an agency, it will do so if it encounters difficulty. The "moral obligation" is critical to the rating agencies' evaluation of debt. S&P says it assesses "the willingness of the federal government to provide support . . . On a stand-alone basis, most (GSEs) would be less than AAA." Agencies most commonly defined as GSEs are the Federal Farm Credit Banks, the Federal Home Loan Banks, the Federal Home Loan Mortgage Corp., the Federal National Mortgage Association, the Student Loan Marketing Association, and, in some instances, Financing Corp., Resolution Funding Corp., and the Tennessee Valley Authority.

Would the U.S. government help a GSE or other agency that could not meet its obligations? Let's look at several examples.

The Farm Credit System

In the 1970s, the agriculture industry boomed and the federal Farm Credit System (FCS) expanded rapidly into the early 1980s. FCS bonds, benefiting from investors' favorable perception, traded very close to Treasury obligations. By 1984, however, system banks began to suffer significant losses and presented the government with a dilemma. Though FCS debt was not an obligation of, or guaranteed by, the United States or any agency other than banks, investors believed FCS bonds were federally guaranteed. If the government did not back the FCS, the mortgage industry could be negatively affected. A 1985 study by Chase Econometrics concluded that investors would perceive greater risk in other "agency" bonds if the government did not step in. This would drive up their cost of borrowing and home mortgage interest rates would have risen from 12.5 percent to 15 percent, or more.[2] Emergency bailout legislation was signed into law in 1988. The Agriculture Credit Act of 1987 created two new entities to assist the troubled institutions, the Farm Credit Assistance Financial Corporation (FAC) and the Federal Agricultural Mortgage Corporation (FAMC, Farmer Mac). Because institutions carry a federal guarantee, the government could explicitly guarantee all obligations issued by the lending institutions that make up the FCS.

Tennessee Valley Authority

Although this agency is wholly owned by the U.S. government, its debt is not a U.S. obligation. Bonds are secured by a first charge upon net power proceeds. The TVA did sell long-term bonds to the Federal Financing Bank (FFB), which is backed by the full faith and credit of the government. After facing 1989 FFB resistance to paying off higher-coupon debt early, the TVA turned to the public market to issue long-term bonds to pay off the debt. While this resulted in significant interest cost savings, the FFB had originally threatened that if the TVA borrowed elsewhere, it might not be permitted to borrow again from the FFB. Before a second TVA public offering, the agencies reached a compromise: TVA could continue to finance via the FFB over a two-year "transition period."

Federal Savings and Loan Insurance Corporation (FSLIC)

The recession of the early 1980s resulted in a crisis that devastated the banking industry. Savings and loan failures hit the nation mid-decade, and FSLIC lacked insurance funds to pay off depositors. In early 1989, the Bush Administration submitted a proposal to Congress to restructure the dated thrift system and rescue depositors at failed institutions. The Financial Institutions Reform, Recovery, and Enforcement Act of 1989 (FIRREA) was signed into law in August. One provision created a new agency, the Resolution Funding Corp. (Refcorp). Refcorp was to provide funding for the Resolution Trust Corp. (RTC), which, in turn, resolved cases involving the sale and deposition of FSLIC-insured institutions and their assets. Refcorp was originally charged to issue $50 billion in long-term bonds for the RTC to meet these obligations.

The U.S. government has demonstrated its ability and willingness to rescue federally related agencies, even if the government does not legislatively guarantee the agency's debt. The rating agencies, while purporting that the implicit/explicit distinction is important, recognize the government's involvement. As S&P stated in February 1991, "Historical statements or examples of federal commitment are important. For example, legislation assisting the Farm Credit System in 1985 and 1987 showed that Congress is ready to stand behind that entity." S&P later concluded that "the weaker the agency/corporation is on its own financial terms, the stronger the government support tends to be."[3]

This implied support presents the government and taxpayers with some dilemmas. First, GSEs have been the capital markets' most rapidly growing borrowers, rivaling Treasury's borrowings. GSEs enjoy low operating costs and a political benefit—their borrowings are not included in the federal budget. Since more than $800 billion of GSE loans and guarantees were outstanding by 1990, this benefit could have serious implications.

Refcorp's relationship to the government is also ambiguous. Refcorp is consistently categorized as a GSE and its bonds are not backed by the full faith and credit of the United States. However, the Treasury is ultimately responsible for making interest payments if other funding sources are not available.

As stated under "Treasury Backup" in FIRREA:

> (i) IN GENERAL—To the extent the amounts available pursuant to subparagraphs (A), (B), (C), and (D) are insufficient to cover the amount of *interest payments*, the Secretary of the Treasury *shall* pay to the Funding Corporation the additional amount due, which shall be used by the Funding Corporation to pay such interest." (emphasis added)

The subsection provides for the appropriation of such funds:

> (iii) APPROPRIATION OF FUNDS—There are hereby appropriated to the Secretary, for fiscal year 1989 and each fiscal year thereafter, such sums as may be necessary to carry out clause (i).

Moreover, the Refcorp Offering Circular describes how Refcorp is required to place with the Federal Reserve as trustee an adequate amount of U.S. Treasury Zero-Coupon Bonds to pay off the full maturity of the bonds when due. Refcorp bonds were originally issued with 30- or 40-year maturities. Reading FIRREA and the Offering Circular makes clear that these bonds are every bit as secure as full faith and credit U.S. Treasuries. If the government can renounce the legislative provisions of Refcorp, could it not renege on Treasuries? Yet, when Refcorp bonds were first marketed, they traded at nearly 30 basis points over comparable Treasuries, and these bonds are also exempt from state taxes like U.S. Treasuries. More recent records show the market now realizes Refcorp's value—the yield differential has dropped to less than 10 basis points. See Figure 8–2.

CONCLUSIONS

From this brief review of the government market we can draw three conclusions. Two of them apply to some extent to the insured versus natural Triple-A municipal market.

Security. On the surface, a security difference exists between full faith and credit instruments and GSE debt. Taken in a vacuum, an agency issue with only moral obligation backing and no credit fundamentals should not enjoy the same rating as the better security of a Treasury bill, bond, or note. On the municipal side, security provisions by bond type tend to be homogeneous. That is, general obligation bonds and full faith and credit instruments, and revenue bonds have a myriad of security provisions. Trading and rating differentials result from investor perception of the security's strength, not from the form the security takes.

Precedent. While government and agency bonds do differ in security, how many GSE bonds have failed to pay? The U.S. government's implied support of GSEs and other agencies has historically resembled a relationship with explicit legal support. For very compelling reasons, the federal government has not allowed a federal agency to default on its obligation to pay its lenders. To this point, the Bureau of National Affairs recently noted:

FIGURE 8–2
Comparative Yields—U.S. Treasuries 8 1/8% due August 2019, Refcorp 8 1/8% due October 2019

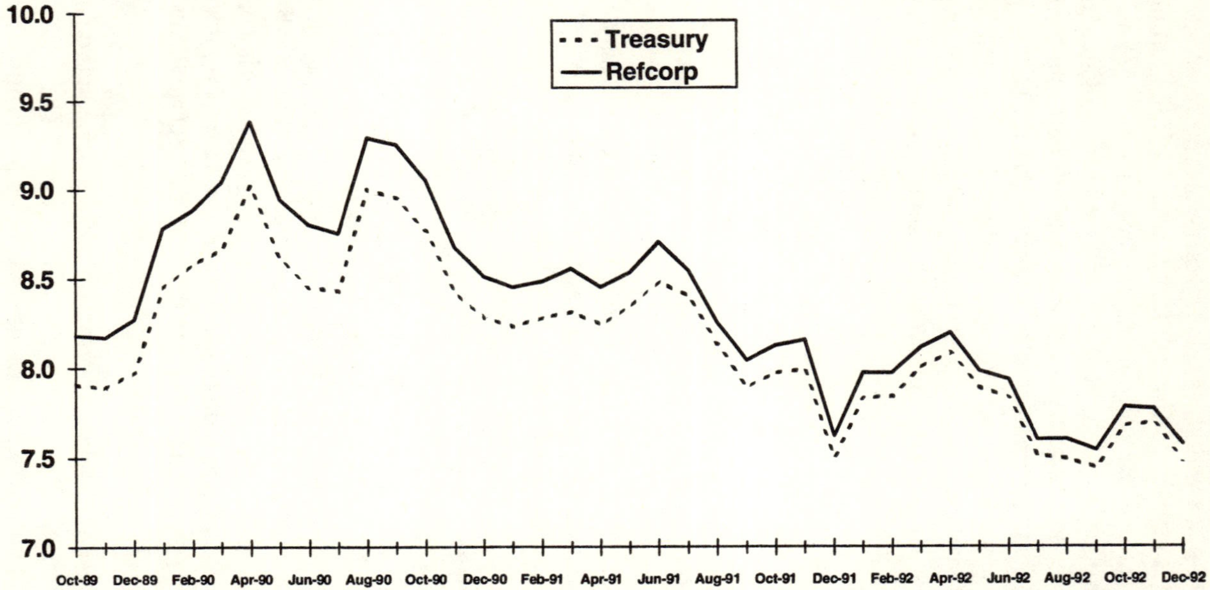

Source: Bloomberg Financial Markets.

> A senate Banking Committee Background paper on GSEs said that 'as a practical matter . . . it is difficult to imagine a failure of one or more of these agencies without a government bailout.'[4]

The value of this history has not been fully exploited for the issuers' benefit.

Confusion. Refcorp is a prime example. Although this agency's bonds had all the trappings of full faith and credit instruments, they initially traded at a far greater yield than Treasuries. Only recently have investors appreciated their value vis-à-vis Treasuries.

Perhaps the government market's greatest lesson is that all bond markets are a vast collection of perceptions, fears, and collective biases that influence trading value. The good news for the seller (and buyer) is that a persistent search, review, and understanding of fact can cure the market inefficiencies these subjective factors create

NOTES

1. Standard & Poor's Corporation, "Agencies with Implied U.S. Support," *Standard & Poor's Creditweek*, February 25, 1991, pp. 39–41.
2. Don Kendall, The Associated Press, November 7, 1985, Section: Washington Dateline (citing study by Chase Econometrics financed by FCS).
3. Standard & Poor's Corporation, "Agencies with Implied U.S. Support," *Standard & Poor's Creditweek*, February 25, 1991, pp. 39–41
4. The Bureau of National Affairs, Inc., *Daily Report for Executives*. Sect: Regulation Economics and Law; DER No.95, May 16, 1990, p. A–9.

CHAPTER 9

CONCLUSIONS

Let us review what we learned and assess how it might affect the members of the bond market. We will summarize our principal findings, analyze them, and conclude with an outlook for the impact.

KEY FINDINGS

Triple-A Is a High Standard. The Triple-A rating category demonstrably consists of institutions that are extremely strong financially. Both major rating agencies created an absolute standard and require members of this elite financial group to maintain strong fundamentals.

Natural Triple-A's Deserve the Rating. Natural Triple-A's have earned the distinction of the rating by their credit fundamentals and financial performance. The standing they enjoy is not misplaced, and even though natural Triple-A's do not undergo the formal, rigorous tests that Triple-A bond insurers undergo, natural bond issuers present a very sound credit picture. However, natural Triple-A's have also benefited from the myth of unlimited taxing power, which leads to the market's lowest bond interest rates. The myth's transitory nature was amply demonstrated when the State of California was downgraded from Triple-A. While California's GNP ranks 17th in the world, it could not summon the political will to keep its lofty rating. In the end, California accepted a lower rating with higher interest payments, rather than require taxpayers to pay more to balance the state budget. The Bond Investors Association observed:

> The California downgrade illustrates a key point we have been making for some time, namely that bonds which carry a natural AAA rating are inferior

> to those which are rated AAA by virtue of the backing of a bond insurer. Although credit agencies rate municipalities based on economic and financial considerations, they cannot fairly assess the biggest risk in municipal general obligation debt, namely political risk. We used California to illustrate this point early in 1991 and now see our prediction borne out.[1]

Insured Bonds Are Better Secured. Insured bonds seem to have suffered unfairly from various degrees of skepticism about their ability to perform as well as natural Triple-A's. For example, they have endured the capital-adequacy allegation that insurers do not have sufficient resources to meet their obligations when the economic chips are down. Our research has shown this is every bit as much a misunderstanding as "unlimited" taxing power. Insured bonds are even stronger than natural Triple-A's because of the extra measure of protection. Recall that the bond issuer itself enjoys relatively good financial attributes or no insurer would guarantee its bonds in the first place. In addition, the insurer's own financial resources come into play if the issuer has problems during the life of a bond issue.

Two protections are better than the one the investor receives from a natural Triple-A. We proved this by applying severe economic pressure to both naturals and insured bonds. A diversified portfolio of natural Triple-A bonds probably would not make it through a Great Depression without defaults. Insured bonds, on the other hand, should do so without any ultimate defaults. The depression stress test the rating agencies apply to bond insurers requires them to have a capital cushion to survive the Great Depression and remain operational. The test gives great protection to holders of insured bonds and assures investors that the extra protection will perform. This is a significant benefit to the smaller bond investor.

When buying natural Triple-A's, the investor must be able to pick bonds most likely to survive severe economic stress, a difficult task since our own testing showed that 39 of the 87 natural Triple-A general obligation and tax-backed issuers would default to some extent in a Great Depression scenario. Bond investors have a dilemma. If they attempt to diversify, they increase the chance of buying a defaulting issue. If they attempt to steer clear of defaults by buying the strongest issues, there is no certainty they will select correctly, or that the issuer's financial condition will not change dramatically at some time in the future. Given this dilemma, investors are wiser to elect extra protection, the "belt and suspenders" support of an investment grade issue backed by insurance.

Marketability and Credit Quality Are Interdependent. Bond marketability cannot be separated from credit quality. Earlier studies said the perception of default risk and bond marketability explained different interest rates. Marketability relates to the scarcity of an issuer's bonds and the size of the issues brought to the market. Our research showed that both the naturals and the insured bonds had strengths as well as weaknesses. But it seemed that the interest rate penalty paid by insured bonds was disproportionate to the weaknesses. We base this finding on the link between marketability and credit quality. Neither scarcity nor attractive issue size alone can make a dubious bond trade significantly better than a quality bond. Bond buyers search first for the best quality, then review the other attributes.

Bond Market Confusion Leads to Rate Differentials. Studying the government bond market was a valuable experience that graphically demonstrated perception-versus-reality problems. The federal government has never allowed any of its agencies—not even those that were not full-faith-and-credit issuers—to default on their obligations. Though tomorrow might bring different results, the long historical record shows that credit risk of an agency bond is the same as that of a United States Treasury bond.

Moreover, the Refcorp example revealed perception-versus-reality problems with two bonds of equal security. The bond market is prone to the forces of fear, bias, prejudice, and misinformation as is any other market, and when such phenomena occur, bargains develop for the bond investor. However, the issuer has to bear the extra cost. Very clearly, issuers must continually communicate about their bonds and address the fears and misunderstandings that arise in the market. Issuers that do the marketing job of assuring that the facts are received and properly interpreted are much more likely to enjoy the rewards of lower interest rates.

EFFECTS OF RESEARCH

What is the likely effect of our findings? Let's place ourselves in the shoes of the major bond market constituents.

Bond Investors. Bond investors that have bought insured bonds in record numbers over the last few years have received one of the better bargains in the fixed income market. The buyer purchased a bond from an issuer that already had generally good underlying credit attributes and financial strength while also receiving access to a strong insurer's balance sheet resources. In addition, these investors were rewarded with *extra* yield of \$1–\$2 per bond per year over natural Triple-A's. It's true the bond buyer could have purchased an uninsured counterpart of the insured bond and received even more yield, but look at what could have happened. For perhaps another dollar per bond per year in yield, the investor in a New York City or Philadelphia bond would have suffered a \$75 dollar per bond drop in value during the fall of 1990 when the effects of the recession in the Northeast and credit problems in Philadelphia, in particular, triggered a drop in the value of these bonds. The extra dollar or two a year in yield would not have compensated buyers who had to sell when the bonds fell.

On the other hand, if the investor had bought a natural Triple-A bond at an even lower yield and given up a dollar or more per bond per year, those holders would have been unprotected if the Triple-A were lost. The State of California is a case in point. Because of the perception of unlimited taxing power, California sold bonds at very low Triple-A interest rates. Now that the rating is gone, the original investors probably will never recover the values lost by the downgrade.

Given the market growth of insured bonds and the demand that fueled that growth, it seems that bond investors knew the bargain they were getting and bought bonds in record numbers. However, bond investors should understand that issuers and bond insurers may seek recognition for the value they provide and try to narrow the yield differential between themselves and their natural counterparts. Bond investors will still get a bargain, though perhaps not as great as they have enjoyed over the past few years. Even so, there's another benefit for the early investor in insured bonds: capital gains resulting from the market's greater appreciation of insured bond quality. What about the other side of the table?

Bond Insurers and Issuers. Bond insurers and issuers have not been left out of the golden age. The extra yield bond investors have gained with insured bonds has come largely from a heretofore unavailable opportunity for bond insurers (and insured issuers) to extract a higher value for their product. To be fair, bond issuers saved substantial sums with bond insurance and bond insurers enjoyed respectable premiums and profits for the undertaking. And, before this study, there was no conclusive proof which was the better bond. However, we believe we have documented that the market has undervalued bond insurance and that insured bonds should trade as well as naturals. To make this happen, bond insurers and issuers must continually communicate to investors the value of their products. Once the value is understood and existing perceptions changed, trading values between natural and insured Triple-A issues will narrow, and issuers who purchase bond insurance will realize even greater interest cost savings.

The value-oriented investing espoused by Benjamin Graham and David Dodd taught equity investors that markets are fickle and that there will always be a time when a dollar is selling for $1.50 or for 50 cents. Studious investors should buy at the latter time and sell at the former. While we did not try to discover a trove of undervalued companies as Graham and Dodd did in the Great Depression, we found under-appreciated and under-valued bonds which shrewd investors can buy for the proverbial 50 cents and even improve their security. These profits will go to the investor who diligently separates myths and perceptions from realities.

NOTE

1. C. Richard Lehmann, Editor, "California Dreaming—No Longer AAA," *Bond Investors Association Newsletter*, March, 1992, p. 1.

BIBLIOGRAPHY

Association of Financial Guaranty Insurors (AFGI). 1991 Annual Report.

Bahl, Roy W. "Measuring the Creditworthiness of State and Local Governments Municipal Bond Ratings." Proceedings of the *National Tax Journal*, September 1971.

Bland, Robert L., and Chilik Yu. "Municipal Bond Insurance: An Assessment of its Effectiveness at Lowering Costs." *Government Finance Review*, June 1987.

Board of Governors of the Federal Reserve System. *Flow of Funds Accounts, Fourth Quarter 1991*, Annual Revisions. Washington, D.C.

Board of Governors of the Federal Reserve System. *Flow of Funds Accounts, Second Quarter 1992*. Washington, D.C.

The Bond Buyer. *The Bond Buyer 1992 Yearbook*. New York: American Banker Bond Buyer, 1992.

The Bond Buyer. New York: American Banker. Bond Buyer, various dates.

Boyle, Nicholas. "Digging Up Bond Insurance's Roots: Many Minds Planted the Same Seeds." *The Bond Buyer 100th Anniversary Edition*, 1991.

The Bureau of National Affairs, Inc. *Daily Report for Executives*, Sect: Regulation Economics and Law; DER No. 95, May 16, 1990.

Carelton, Willard T., and Eugene M. Lerner. "Statistical Credit Scoring of Municipal Bonds." *Journal of Money, Credit and Banking*, November 1969.

Davidson, R.B. III. "Analyzing Municipal Quality Spreads," *Municipal Finance Journal*, 12, no. 3, Fall 1991.

The First Boston Corporation. *Handbook of U.S. Government and Federal Agency Securities and Related Money Market Instruments, 34th ed.* Chicago, IL: Probus Publishing, 1990.

Gastel, Ruth (ed.). *Financial Guarantee Insurance*. New York: Insurance Information Institute, 1986.

Godfrey, Robert R. *Risk Based Capital Charges for Municipal Bonds*. Greenwich, CT: JAI Press Inc., 1990.

Hastie, K. Larry. "Determinants of Municipal Bond Yields." *Journal of Finance and Quantitative Analysis*, June 1972.

Heimowitz, Daniel, and Edward Kerman. "Aaa Bonds," Moody's Investors Service—*Municipal Issues*, Nov./Dec. 1989.

Hempel, George H. *The Postwar Quality of State and Local Debt.* National Bureau of Economic Research. New York: Columbia University Press, 1971.

The Heritage Foundation. "The Federal Government's Credit Obligations," *Heritage Foundation Reports*, June 28, 1990, Sect. No. 774.

Hickman, W. Braddock. *The Volume of Corporate Bond Financing Since 1900.* National Bureau of Economic Research. Princeton, NJ: Princeton University Press, 1953.

Kendall, Don. The Associated Press, November 7, 1985, Section: Washington Dateline (citing study by Chase Econometrics financed by FCS).

Kreps, Matthew. "Ups and Downs of Municipal Bonds' Volume and Yield in the Past Century." *The Bond Buyer 100th Anniversary Edition*, 1991.

Lehmann, C. Richard. "California Dreaming—No Longer AAA." *Bond Investors Association Newsletter*, March 1992.

McGoldrick, Beth. "The Return of TVA," *Institutional Investor*, January 1990.

Moody's Investors Service. "$5.6 Billion Affected by Second Quarter Municipal Bond Rating Revisions." *Moody's Public Finance Dept. Rating News*, July 10, 1992.

Moody's Investors Service. *Moody's Bond Record.* New York: Moody's Investors Service, various editions.

Moody's Investors Service. *Moody's Municipal Credit Report*—State of California, October 29, 1991.

Moody's Investors Service. *Moody's on Municipals.* New York: Moody's Investors Service, Inc., 1991.

Moody's Investors Service. *Moody's Municipal and Government Manual.* New York: Moody's Investors Service, 1991.

Moody's Investors Service. *Moody's Special Comment: U.S. Government-Sponsored Enterprises (GSEs).* February 1990.

Moody's Investors Service. "Municipal Bond Rating Revisions–1991." *Moody's Municipal Credit Report*, January 1992.

Moody's Investors Service, Public Finance Dept. *Municipal Focus on Counties*, July 1991.

Mysak, Joe. "Bond Insurer Halts Guarantees through Its HIBI Program." *The Bond Buyer*, September 24, 1985.

Standard & Poor's Corporation. "Agencies with Implied U.S. Support." *Standard & Poor's Creditweek*, February 25, 1991.

Standard & Poor's Corporation. "Federally Related Bonds: A Discussion of Terms." *Standard & Poor's Creditweek*, July 1, 1991.

Standard & Poor's Corporation. "Muni Downgrades Fell Sharply in Second Quarter." *Standard & Poor's Creditweek*, July 20, 1992.

Standard & Poor's Corporation. "Municipal Insurers' Staying Power Debated." *Standard & Poor's Credit Review*, November 26, 1990.

Standard & Poor's Corporation. "Municipal Ratings Hit Hard." *Standard & Poor's Credit Review*, February 3, 1992.

Standard & Poor's Corporation. "Rating Methodology." *Standard & Poor's Credit Review—Bond Insurance*, December 15, 1986.

Standard & Poor's Corporation. "Ratings Lowered on $5.2 Billion of Insured Debt." *Standard & Poor's Creditweek*, December 23, 1985.

Standard & Poor's Corporation. *S&P's Municipal Finance Criteria*. New York: Standard & Poor's Corp., 1989.

Standard & Poor's Corporation. "USF&G's Claims-Paying Ability Cut to 'AA,'" *Standard & Poor's Creditweek*, April 28, 1986.

Standard & Poor's Insurance Rating Services. *S&P's Insurer Ratings List Claims-Paying Ability*, February 1992.

DATA TABLES

Interest Rates and Spreads Between Natural Triple-A and Insured Municipal Bonds

	Natural AAA	*Insured AAA*	*Spread*
Jan-87	6.09	6.85	0.76
Feb-87	6.05	6.83	0.78
Mar-87	6.25	6.90	0.65
Apr-87	7.15	7.74	0.59
May-87	7.57	8.11	0.54
Jun-87	7.44	7.83	0.39
Jul-87	7.18	7.90	0.72
Aug-87	7.24	7.89	0.65
Sep-87	7.67	8.33	0.65
Oct-87	7.90	8.65	0.75
Nov-87	7.50	8.15	0.65
Dec-87	7.45	8.16	0.71
Jan-88	7.31	7.79	0.48
Feb-88	7.05	7.58	0.53
Mar-88	7.14	7.85	0.71
Apr-88	7.35	7.98	0.63
May-88	7.57	8.03	0.46
Jun-88	7.51	7.88	0.37
Jul-88	7.50	7.86	0.36
Aug-88	7.51	7.91	0.40
Sep-88	7.39	7.76	0.37
Oct-88	7.25	7.56	0.31
Nov-88	7.35	7.58	0.23
Dec-88	7.35	7.66	0.31
Jan-89	7.23	7.36	0.13
Feb-89	7.23	7.50	0.27
Mar-89	7.40	7.66	0.26
Apr-89	7.37	7.53	0.16
May-89	7.22	7.23	0.01
Jun-89	6.79	7.12	0.33
Jul-89	6.69	7.09	0.40
Aug-89	6.68	7.11	0.43
Sep-89	6.90	7.26	0.36
Oct-89	6.93	7.21	0.28
Nov-89	6.79	7.15	0.36
Dec-89	6.71	7.06	0.35

Jan-90	6.81	7.16	0.35
Feb-90	7.05	7.21	0.16
Mar-90	6.98	7.23	0.25
Apr-90	7.04	7.28	0.24
May-90	7.07	7.28	0.21
Jun-90	6.88	7.21	0.33
Jul-90	6.96	7.15	0.19
Aug-90	6.99	7.31	0.32
Sep-90	7.18	7.43	0.25
Oct-90	7.24	7.49	0.25
Nov-90	6.75	7.14	0.39
Dec-90	6.63	7.08	0.45
Jan-91	6.57	7.05	0.48
Feb-91	6.41	6.88	0.47
Mar-91	6.76	6.98	0.22
Apr-91	6.70	6.95	0.25
May-91	6.70	6.92	0.22
Jun-91	6.83	7.03	0.20
Jul-91	6.82	6.93	0.11
Aug-91	6.62	6.86	0.24
Sep-91	6.51	6.83	0.32
Oct-91	6.28	6.73	0.45
Nov-91	6.24	6.70	0.46
Dec-91	6.32	6.65	0.33
Jan-92	6.13	6.49	0.36
Feb-92	6.30	6.58	0.28
Mar-92	6.45	6.65	0.20
Apr-92	6.36	6.58	0.22
May-92	6.25	6.49	0.24
Jun-92	6.19	6.42	0.23
Jul-92	5.72	6.05	0.33
Aug-92	5.67	6.13	0.46
Sep-92	5.92	6.21	0.29
Oct-92	6.10	6.38	0.28
Nov-92	6.08	6.33	0.25
Dec-92	5.91	6.21	0.30

Sources: Natural Aaa-Moody's Municipal and Government Manual;
Moody's Bond Record;
Insured AAA - Smith Barney Credit Market Comment.

Number of Municipal Bond Defaults 1869-1991

Year	Defaults	Year	Defaults	Year	Defaults
1869	0	1910	2	1951	11
1870	14	1911	9	1952	54
1871	7	1912	6	1953	0
1872	11	1913	1	1954	7
1873	19	1914	4	1955	4
1874	11	1915	5	1956	4
1875	11	1916	0	1957	0
1876	29	1917	0	1958	7
1877	24	1918	1	1959	11
1878	25	1919	8	1960	0
1879	17	1920	4	1961	0
1880	26	1921	11	1962	38
1881	13	1922	9	1963	77
1882	7	1923	7	1964	0
1883	7	1924	11	1965	77
1884	13	1925	40	1966	26
1885	7	1926	9	1967	8
1886	4	1927	59	1968	51
1887	5	1928	14	1969	17
1888	5	1929	22	1970	1
1889	10	1930	121	1971	3
1890	12	1931	302	1972	3
1891	9	1932	493	1973	5
1892	18	1933	1,590	1974	11
1893	13	1934	1,409	1975	11
1894	16	1935	638	1976	17
1895	30	1936	160	1977	11
1896	41	1937	36	1978	26
1897	45	1938	11	1979	2
1898	58	1939	10	1980	2
1899	16	1940	38	1981	7
1900	19	1941	7	1982	16
1901	33	1942	16	1983	25
1902	23	1943	5	1984	47
1903	19	1944	2	1985	56

1904	21	1945	3	1986	150
1905	17	1946	3	1987	175
1906	9	1947	2	1988	139
1907	5	1948	2	1989	105
1908	1	1949	1	1990	162
1909	2	1950	14	1991	252

Sources: Risk Based Capital Charges For Municipal Bonds (JAI Press-1990); Bond Investors Association.

Individuals as Holders of Total Municipal Debt Outstanding ($ in Billions)

	Total Tax-Exempt Debt Outstanding ($)	*Individual Owned (%)*	*Tax-Exempt Debt Held By Individuals ($)*
1982	451	38.64	175
1983	506	44.04	223
1984	564	47.29	267
1985	743	50.44	375
1986	790	54.94	434
1987	873	60.69	530
1988	939	64.87	609
1989	1,004	68.66	690
1990	1,050	70.67	742
1991	1,101	72.13	806

Source: Fed Flow of Funds.

New Issue Municipal Bonds
Insured Municipal Bonds - Natural Triple-A Bonds
($ in Millions)

	Total ($)	*Insd/Total (%)*	*Insd ($)*	*Nat AAA ($)*	*Nat/Total (%)*
1971	24,370	0.01	2.150		
1972	22,941	0.13	30.738		
1973	22,953	0.01	1.150		
1974	22,824	0.49	110.925		
1975	29,326	1.90	557.978		
1976	33,845	2.68	905.717		
1977	45,060	2.70	1,215.257		
1978	46,215	2.22	1,027.616		
1979	42,261	1.68	711.179		
1980	47,133	3.15	1,486.000		
1981	46,134	6.20	2,859.000		
1982	77,179	8.66	6,681.000		
1983	83,348	15.07	12,558.000		
1984	101,881	15.85	16,145.000		
1985	206,991	20.96	43,378.000		
1986	151,258	14.25	21,558.000		
1987	105,439	17.77	18,737.000		
1988	117,190	21.82	25,570.000		
1989	124,954	23.32	29,138.000	5,368	4.40
1990	127,938	26.44	33,829.000	6,778	5.60
1991	172,576	29.95	51,688.000	9,958	6.10
1992	232,281	34.52	80,178.000	4,394**	4.10
*1993	64,611	36.82	23,788.000		
Total	1,948,708	19.10	372,155.710		

* First 4 months

** 6 months

Source: Bond Buyer/MBIA Database.

Outstanding Number of Triple-A Issuers

	Moody's	*Standard & Poor's*
1971	71	120
1972	77	108
1973	104	104
1974	123	98
1975	135	87
1976	136	81
1977	141	77
1978	137	83
1979	139	78
1980	133	78
1981	134	76
1982	115	77
1983	107	64
1984	105	65
1985	103	64
1986	107	61
1987	106	58
1988	116	59
1989	123	59
1990	125	60
1991	126	57

Sources: Moody's Reports
Standard & Poor's Reports

Triple-A Rating Actions

	Standard & Poor's		Moody's	
	Withdrawn/ Downgrades	*New Issues/ Upgrades*	*Withdrawn/ Downgrades*	*New Issues/ Upgrades*
1971	0		0	
1972	-15	3	-4	10
1973	-9	5	-2	29
1974	-15	9	-5	24
1975	-17	6	-5	17
1976	-12	6	-6	7
1977	-8	4	-2	9
1978	-2	8	-9	5
1979	-5	0	-2	4
1980	-3	3	-7	1
1981	-2	0	-3	4
1982	-3	4	-21	2
1983	-16	3	-9	1
1984	0	1	-4	2
1985	-4	3	-3	1
1986	-6	3	-4	8
1987	-6	3	-11	7
1988	-2	3	-2	12
1989	-1	1	-1	8
1990	-1	2	-2	4
1991	-3	0	-2	3

Sources: Standard & Poor's Reports
Moody's Reports

Key Economic Variables
State & Local Government
($ in Billions)

	Debt Outstanding	*Revenues*	*Surplus (Deficit)*
1869	-	-	-
1870	0.9	-	-
1871	-	-	-
1872	-	-	-
1873	-	-	-
1874	-	-	-
1875	-	-	-
1876	-	-	-
1877	-	-	-
1878	-	-	-
1879	-	-	-
1880	1.1	-	-
1881	-	-	-
1882	-	-	-
1883	-	-	-
1884	-	-	-
1885	-	-	-
1886	-	-	-
1887	-	-	-
1888	-	-	-
1889	-	-	-
1890	1.1	-	-
1891	-	-	-
1892	-	-	-
1893	-	-	-
1894	-	-	-
1895	-	-	-
1896	-	-	-
1897	-	-	-
1898	-	-	-
1899	-	-	-
1900	-	-	-
1901	-	-	-

1902	1.9	1.0	-
1903	-	-	-
1904	-	-	-
1905	-	-	-
1906	-	-	-
1907	-	-	-
1908	-	-	-
1909	-	-	-
1910	-	-	-
1911	-	-	-
1912	3.8	-	-
1913	-	2.0	-
1914	-	-	-
1915	-	-	-
1916	4.5	-	-
1917	4.8	-	-
1918	5.1	-	-
1919	5.5	-	-
1920	6.2	-	-
1921	7.0	-	-
1922	7.9	5.2	-
1923	8.6	-	-
1924	9.4	-	-
1925	10.3	-	-
1926	11.1	-	-
1927	12.1	7.8	-
1928	12.7	-	-
1929	13.6	7.6	-0.2
1930	14.7	7.8	-0.6
1931	16.0	7.7	-0.8
1932	16.6	7.3	-0.3
1933	16.3	7.2	-0.1
1934	15.9	8.6	0.5
1935	16.1	9.1	0.6
1936	16.2	8.6	0.5
1937	16.1	9.1	0.7
1938	16.1	9.3	0.4
1939	16.4	9.6	0.0

1940	16.4	10.0	0.6
1941	16.1	10.4	1.3
1942	15.4	10.6	1.8
1943	14.5	10.9	2.4
1944	13.9	11.1	2.7
1945	13.4	11.6	2.6
1946	13.7	13.0	1.9
1947	15.0	15.4	1.0
1948	17.0	17.7	0.1
1949	19.1	19.5	-0.7
1950	21.7	21.3	-1.2
1951	24.2	23.4	-0.4
1952	27.0	25.4	0.0
1953	30.7	27.4	0.1
1954	35.5	29.0	-1.1
1955	41.1	31.7	-1.3
1956	44.5	35.0	-0.9
1957	48.6	38.5	-1.4
1958	53.7	42.0	-2.4
1959	59.6	46.6	-0.4
1960	64.9	50.0	0.1
1961	70.5	54.1	-0.4
1962	77.0	58.6	0.5
1963	83.9	63.4	0.5
1964	90.4	69.8	1.0
1965	98.3	75.5	0.0
1966	110.0	85.2	0.5
1967	117.4	94.1	-1.1
1968	126.1	107.9	0.1
1969	138.3	120.8	1.5
1970	150.3	135.8	1.8
1971	166.7	153.6	2.6
1972	180.7	179.3	13.5
1973	194.8	196.4	13.5
1974	208.2	213.1	7.2
1975	219.4	239.6	4.5
1976	233.4	270.1	15.2
1977	242.3	300.1	26.9

1978	284.3	330.3	28.9
1979	299.5	355.3	27.6
1980	310.4	361.4	26.8
1981	326.7	390.8	28.5
1982	357.1	409.0	26.9
1983	391.7	443.5	40.3
1984	427.4	492.2	58.1
1985	561.4	528.7	56.1
1986	620.6	571.3	54.4
1987	703.6	594.3	40.1
1988	752.5	631.3	38.4
1989	815.7	681.5	44.8
1990	864.0	729.3	30.1
1991	902.5	777.8	17.2
1992	950.6	838.0	15.5

- = not available

Sources: Risk Based Capital Charges For Municipal Bonds (JAI Press-1990);
Board of Governors of the Federal Reserve System-
Flow of Funds Accounts Financial Assets and Liabilities
Year-End 1966-1989, Sept. 90;
Flow of Funds Accounts Flows and Outstandings 4Q92.

State and Local Government

	Debt to Revenue Ratio	Surplus to Revenue (%)
1922	1.53	-
1923	-	-
1924	-	-
1925	-	-
1926	-	-
1927	1.54	-
1928	-	-
1929	1.79	-2.6
1930	1.88	-7.7
1931	2.08	-10.3
1932	2.27	-4.1
1933	2.26	-1.3
1934	1.85	5.8
1935	1.77	6.5
1936	1.88	5.8
1937	1.87	7.6
1938	1.73	4.3
1939	1.70	-
1940	1.64	6.0
1941	1.54	12.5
1942	1.45	17.0
1943	1.33	22.0
1944	1.25	24.3
1945	1.15	22.5
1946	1.05	14.7
1947	0.97	6.5
1948	0.98	0.57
1949	0.98	-3.5
1950	1.01	-5.6
1951	1.03	-1.7
1952	1.06	-
1953	1.12	0.37
1954	1.22	-3.7
1955	1.30	-4.1
1956	1.27	-2.6
1957	1.26	-3.6
1958	1.28	-5.7

1959	1.28	-0.9
1960	1.30	0.2
1961	1.30	0.74
1962	1.31	0.85
1963	1.32	0.79
1964	1.29	1.4
1965	1.30	-
1966	1.29	0.59
1967	1.25	-1.1
1968	1.17	0.1
1969	1.14	1.2
1970	1.11	1.3
1971	1.08	1.7
1972	1.01	7.5
1973	0.99	6.9
1974	0.98	3.4
1975	0.92	1.9
1976	0.86	5.7
1977	0.81	8.9
1978	0.86	8.8
1979	0.84	7.7
1980	0.86	6.9
1981	0.84	7.3
1982	0.87	6.6
1983	0.88	9.1
1984	0.87	11.8
1985	1.06	10.6
1986	1.09	9.5
1987	1.18	6.7
1988	1.20	6.1
1989	1.20	6.6
1990	1.18	4.1
1991	1.16	2.2
1992	1.13	1.8

Sources: Risk Based Capital Charges For Municipal Bonds (JAI Press-1990);
Board of Govenors of the Federal Reserve:
Flow of Funds Accounts Financial;
Assets and Liabilities 1966-1989, Sept. 90;
Flows and Outstandings 4Q92.

Personal Income 1929-1991
($ in Billions)

1929	84.30	1961	426.00
1930	75.50	1962	453.20
1931	64.70	1963	476.30
1932	49.40	1964	510.20
1934	46.30	1965	552.00
1935	53.10	1966	600.80
1936	59.80	1967	644.50
1937	68.00	1968	707.20
1938	73.40	1969	772.90
1939	67.60	1970	831.80
1940	72.10	1971	894.00
1941	77.60	1972	981.60
1942	95.20	1973	1,101.70
1943	122.40	1974	1,210.10
1944	150.70	1975	1,313.40
1945	170.00	1976	1,451.40
1946	177.60	1977	1,607.50
1947	190.20	1978	1,812.40
1948	209.20	1979	2,034.00
1949	206.40	1980	2,258.50
1950	228.10	1981	2,520.90
1951	256.50	1982	2,670.80
1952	273.80	1983	2,838.60
1953	290.50	1984	3,108.70
1954	293.00	1985	3,325.30
1955	314.20	1986	3,526.20
1956	337.20	1987	3,777.60
1957	356.30	1988	4,064.50
1958	367.10	1989	4,380.20
1959	390.70	1990	4,679.80
1960	409.40	1991	4,834.40

Sources: Fed Flow of Funds;
U.S. Bureau of Census.

US Treasury vs. Government Mortgage Backed Yields
30 Year Maturity

	GNMA	*FNMA*	*FHLMC*	*TREASURY*
Jan-85	12.326	12.415	12.342	11.200
Feb-85	13.046	13.218	13.135	11.890
Mar-85	12.839	12.927	12.783	11.690
Apr-85	12.557	12.694	12.623	11.390
May-85	11.508	11.402	11.590	10.680
Jun-85	11.293	11.372	11.311	10.550
Jul-85	11.571	11.737	11.672	10.610
Aug-85	11.400	11.696	11.610	10.350
Sep-85	11.472	11.665	11.600	10.480
Oct-85	11.233	11.321	11.240	10.290
Nov-85	10.674	10.762	10.727	9.890
Dec-85	9.835	9.900	10.071	9.290
Jan-86	10.004	10.245	10.195	9.340
Feb-86	9.245	9.400	9.553	8.300
Mar-86	8.930	9.222	9.201	7.780
Apr-86	8.856	9.194	9.174	7.630
May-86	9.859	10.017	10.090	7.710
Jun-86	9.706	9.900	9.836	7.340
Jul-86	9.433	9.738	9.675	7.440
Aug-86	8.833	9.129	9.091	7.250
Sep-86	9.315	9.334	9.303	7.630
Oct-86	9.157	9.203	9.164	7.600
Nov-86	8.292	8.607	8.574	7.410
Dec-86	8.665	8.761	8.709	7.450
Jan-87	8.207	8.327	8.511	7.440
Feb-87	8.247	8.382	8.520	7.490
Mar-87	8.633	8.716	8.700	7.550
Apr-87	9.744	9.766	9.712	8.440
May-87	9.989	10.167	10.109	8.700
Jun-87	9.835	9.871	9.836	8.390
Jul-87	9.916	9.881	9.855	8.820
Aug-87	10.195	10.148	10.128	9.100
Sep-87	10.923	10.812	10.767	9.670
Oct-87	10.307	10.352	10.282	9.050

Nov-87	10.263	10.225	10.176	9.050
Dec-87	10.224	10.196	10.157	8.890
Jan-88	9.490	9.409	9.562	8.490
Feb-88	9.414	9.371	9.525	8.410
Mar-88	9.840	9.719	9.693	8.770
Apr-88	10.157	9.939	10.042	9.080
May-88	10.356	10.249	10.215	9.300
Jun-88	9.955	9.862	9.803	8.850
Jul-88	10.224	10.210	10.123	9.260
Aug-88	10.321	10.283	10.253	9.450
Sep-88	9.975	9.896	9.874	9.070
Oct-88	9.712	9.676	9.656	8.830
Nov-88	10.171	10.148	10.142	9.100
Dec-88	10.410	10.416	10.580	9.000
Jan-89	10.278	10.215	10.234	8.800
Feb-89	10.664	10.658	10.658	9.150
Mar-89	10.778	10.822	10.811	9.160
Apr-89	10.674	10.668	10.663	8.900
May-89	10.147	10.143	10.138	8.660
Jun-89	9.650	9.719	9.708	8.080
Jul-89	9.203	9.250	9.234	8.030
Aug-89	9.792	9.814	9.817	8.200
Sep-89	9.870	9.860	9.930	8.240
Oct-89	9.360	9.420	9.520	7.880
Nov-89	9.310	9.390	9.470	7.890
Dec-89	9.350	9.460	9.540	7.960
Jan-90	9.800	9.850	9.860	8.460
Feb-90	9.880	9.880	9.880	8.550
Mar-90	9.940	9.930	9.930	8.580
Apr-90	10.380	10.370	10.350	9.030
May-90	9.880	9.830	9.930	8.570
Jun-90	9.770	9.740	9.730	8.440
Jul-90	9.430	9.460	9.510	8.530
Aug-90	9.880	9.830	9.830	8.970
Sep-90	9.890	9.820	9.820	9.020
Oct-90	9.830	9.740	9.790	8.730
Nov-90	9.410	9.540	9.530	8.470
Dec-90	9.220	9.290	9.270	8.250

Jan-91	9.030	9.160	9.110	8.200
Feb-91	9.010	9.110	9.080	8.180
Mar-91	9.050	9.600	9.080	8.250
Apr-91	9.000	9.090	9.070	8.230
May-91	9.020	9.040	9.010	8.220
Jun-91	9.260	9.320	9.240	8.480
Jul-91	9.000	9.070	8.960	8.380
Aug-91	8.540	8.690	8.650	7.980
Sep-91	8.320	8.420	8.350	7.880
Oct-91	8.020	8.100	8.130	7.900
Nov-91	8.270	8.300	8.230	7.960
Dec-91	7.370	7.570	7.550	7.500
Jan-92	8.230	8.330	8.300	7.770
Feb-92	8.130	8.190	8.130	7.850
Mar-92	8.430	8.510	8.500	7.970
Apr-92	8.330	8.350	8.220	8.040
May-92	8.190	8.210	8.080	7.850
Jun-92	7.810	7.860	7.810	7.760
Jul-92	7.360	7.520	7.360	7.430
Aug-92	7.340	7.350	7.420	7.400
Sep-92	7.280	7.420	7.340	7.410
Oct-92	7.820	7.880	7.700	7.590
Nov-92	7.860	8.010	7.810	7.530
Dec-92	7.590	7.570	7.430	7.370

Sources: Bloomberg Financial Markets; The Bond Buyer.

Comparative Yields
US Treasuries 8 1/8% Due 8/19
Refcorp 8 1/8% Due 10/19

	Treasury	*Refcorp*		*Treasury*	*Refcorp*
Oct-89	7.91	8.18	Jun-91	8.48	8.70
Nov-89	7.89	8.17	Jul-91	8.40	8.54
Dec-89	7.98	8.27	Aug-91	8.13	8.25
Jan-90	8.45	8.78	Sep-91	7.89	8.04
Feb-90	8.58	8.88	Oct-91	7.97	8.12
Mar-90	8.66	9.04	Nov-91	7.99	8.15
Apr-90	9.02	9.38	Dec-91	7.50	7.62
May-90	8.61	8.94	Jan-92	7.83	7.97
Jun-90	8.45	8.80	Feb-92	7.84	7.97
Jul-90	8.43	8.75	Mar-92	8.00	8.11
Aug-90	9.00	9.29	Apr-92	8.08	8.19
Sep-90	8.95	9.25	May-92	7.89	7.98
Oct-90	8.77	9.05	Jun-92	7.83	7.93
Nov-90	8.42	8.67	Jul-92	7.51	7.60
Dec-90	8.28	8.51	Aug-92	7.49	7.60
Jan-91	8.23	8.45	Sep-92	7.44	7.54
Feb-91	8.28	8.48	Oct-92	7.68	7.78
Mar-91	8.31	8.55	Nov-92	7.69	7.77
Apr-91	8.24	8.45	Dec-92	7.48	7.57
May-91	8.34	8.53			

Source: Bloomberg Financial Markets

Supplemental Credit Comparisons (Related to Table 5-8)

Difference in Means Test for Natural Triple A's and Insured Bonds
Formula

$$t = \frac{\text{Mean (Naturals)} - \text{Mean (Insureds)}}{\sqrt{\dfrac{\text{Standard deviation (naturals)}^2}{\text{Number of observations(naturals)}} + \dfrac{\text{Standard deviation (insureds)}^2}{\text{Number of observations(insureds)}}}}$$

If t is greater than or equal to ± 2.0, the difference in means of the 2 samples is statistically signficant and not so at values less than ± 2.0.

Gross State and Local Debt/Capita

Natural - Mean = $573
Insured - Mean = $1,543
Natural - Standard deviation = $396.23
Insured - Standard deviation = $63.57
$t = -2.42$; Significant

Personal Income/Capita

Natural - Mean = $24,174
Insured - Mean = $29,763
Natural - Standard deviation = $8,258.66
Insured - Standard deviation = $1,366.44
$t = -0.67$; Not significant

Gross State and Local Government Debt to Personal Income Percentage

Natural - Mean = 2.4%
Insured - Mean = 5.1%
Natural - Standard deviation = 1.830%
Insured - Standard deviation = 0.170%
$t = -1.35$; Not significant

Gross State and Local Government Debt to Revenue Ratio

Natural - Mean = 1.10:1
Insured - Mean = 1.16:1
Natural - Standard deviation = 0.11:1
Insured - Standard deviation = 0.79:1
$t = -0.07$; Not significant

INDEX